921
RIPKEN   Gutman, Dan

        Cal Ripken, Jr.,
        my story

DUE DATE   **BRODART**   **09/99**   **16.99**

CAL RIPKEN, JR.
My Story

CAL RIPKEN, JR.

My Story

by **Cal Ripken, Jr.,**
and **Mike Bryan**

ADAPTED BY **DAN GUTMAN**

Dial Books for Young Readers
New York

Published by Dial Books for Young Readers
A division of Penguin Putnam Inc.
345 Hudson Street • New York, New York 10014

Adapted from *The Only Way I Know* by Cal Ripken, Jr.,
with Mike Bryan, published by Viking Penguin
Copyright © Cal Ripken, Jr., 1997, 1998.

Designed by Pamela Darcy
Page 115 constitutes an extension of this copyright page
Printed in the U.S.A. on acid-free paper
First Edition • 10 9 8 7 6 5 4 3 2 1

Library of Congress Cataloging in Publication Data
Gutman, Dan.
Cal Ripken, Jr.: my story/by Cal Ripken, Jr., and Mike Bryan;
adapted by Dan Gutman.
p.   cm.
Adaptation of: The only way I know/Cal Ripken, Jr.,
and Mike Bryan. 1997.
Summary: Tells, in his own words, the story of the personal life and
baseball career of the star player for the Baltimore Orioles, Cal Ripken.
ISBN 0-8037-2348-2
1. Ripken, Cal, 1960-   —Juvenile literature. 2. Baseball players—
United States—Biography—Juvenile literature. 3. Baltimore Orioles
(Baseball team)—Juvenile literature. [1. Ripken, Cal, 1960-   . 2. Baseball
players.] I. Ripken, Cal, 1960-   . Only way I know.
II. Bryan, Mike. III. Title.
GV865.R47G89   1999   796.357'092—dc21   [b]   98-7799   CIP   AC

FOR MY FAMILY, WHO SHOWS ME THE WAY

Contents

CAL RIPKEN, JR.
My Story

Introduction

Imagine this—all your childhood you dream of playing in the big leagues. You play your heart out in Little League and high school baseball. You get to be a pretty good player. You reach the minors.

Then, finally, the phone rings one day. You've been called up to play for the Baltimore Orioles.

And you sit on the bench.

That's what happened to me in 1981. My father was the Orioles' third-base coach at the time, but I knew that wasn't going to help me win a spot in the lineup. That's not the way it works in baseball. You have to prove yourself. And you can't prove yourself until somebody gives you a chance.

So I sat on that bench chewing sunflower seeds most of the summer. I kept wondering—how can I ever break into this lineup? And if I do, how can I *stay* there?

I came up with two answers: *play well* and *play every day*.

When I get my shot, I decided, I'm going to play so *well* that the manager won't have any choice but to put my name on his lineup card every day.

And you know what? It worked. I became a regular on opening day of 1982. And as of May 30, 1982, my name was on that lineup card every game for the rest of that season, and for the next sixteen seasons. In September of 1995 I played my 2,131st straight game to break the great Lou Gehrig's record. And in September of 1998, I played my 2,632nd consecutive game.

But I didn't break that record because of my incredible talent or my bionic body. I don't have either of those.

And I didn't play all those games just for the sake of getting my name in the record books.

It was much simpler than that. All I ever wanted to do was play well and play every day.

During my career, I've been to the World Series. I've also played in some great seasons and some not-so-great seasons. I've played alongside Hall of Famers, and I've played with guys who would never reach the majors. I've been praised and I've been criticized. I've hit hundreds of home runs, and I've struck out hundreds of times.

It's been an adventure. And I've played it one game at a time. That's my style. It's the only way I know.

1 · Childhood

When I was born on August 24, 1960, I weighed in at nine pounds and two ounces. A *big* baby!

My dad, Cal Ripken, Sr., was a catcher in the minor leagues at the time. One of his teammates, Boog Powell, heard about me—this gigantic infant—and joked, "He must have been born wearing his catcher's gear!"

Dad was a good player. He hit .281 the year I was born, with nine homers and seventy-four RBIs. But the next spring, he got hit on his right shoulder by two straight foul tips. It messed up his throwing arm pretty badly.

These days, doctors can fix an injury like that in months. But back in the early sixties, it took years to heal. So Dad shifted his sights from playing ball to coaching and managing.

Dad managed for several teams in the Orioles

organization, so the whole family traveled with him. That included my mom, Violet, my older sister, Ellen, my younger brothers, Fred and Billy, and our dog, Scooby.

These are the towns we lived in during my first eighteen years: Phoenix, Arizona . . . Wilson, North Carolina . . . Pensacola, Florida . . . Amarillo, Texas . . . Appleton, Wisconsin . . . Little Rock, Arkansas . . . Leesburg, Florida . . . Rochester, New York . . . Aberdeen, South Dakota . . . Tri Cities, Washington . . . Miami, Florida . . . Elmira, New York . . . Dallas, Texas . . . Asheville, North Carolina . . . But home was always Aberdeen, Maryland. It was not your typical childhood, as you can imagine.

Every February we would load up Dad's blue Buick station wagon and hitch up a trailer behind it. We brought everything with us—household items, our bikes strapped to the roof, even our swing set. Then we'd head to Florida for spring training.

A month later we'd load it all up again and head for whatever town Dad would be working in that summer.

I remember those long car rides. Sometimes we kids would put plastic army helmets on and hang our heads out the window. Naturally, the helmets would blow off. Sometimes Dad would turn the car around to go get them. Other times he would reach back over his seat to "correct" one or more of us crammed into the backseat.

Traveling around so much meant that school

could sometimes be a bit confusing. Some years we would miss a week going to or from spring training. In first grade I would wait until my teacher, Mrs. St. Pierre, was distracted. Then I would get my coat from the closet and just bolt for the door. I did this a few times.

Mom thought about holding me back a year, but I finally settled in with the help of Mrs. St. Pierre, who was really nice and took a special interest in me.

Missing some school here or there wasn't a big problem. I would always make it up. The tough part about traveling from town to town every year was trying to make friends. The Ripken kids relied mainly on each other for friendship.

One time, in Miami, we got into a rotten mango-throwing fight with some neighborhood kids. In Rochester some local kids started making fun of my dad's losing streak, and it turned into a rock-throwing war.

Most of the time, though, we competed against each *other*. Elly, as Ellen was always called, and Fred, Billy, and I all loved sports. We'd play baseball, basketball, soccer, Ping-Pong, bowling—any game, really. We broke so many windows in the garage that Dad taught us how to cut and install new panes of glass. Finally, he got fed up and switched to Plexiglas.

I was as competitive as anyone. One day I was playing checkers and made a quadruple jump. When I leaped up with joy, I slammed my head against the windowsill. The result was a trip to the emergency room and five stitches.

I was a bad loser and a bad winner too. Sometimes, I must admit, I resorted to cheating to beat my brothers and sister. For years I kept detailed statistics on all the family games, just so that I could prove I was best. Eventually I figured out that the only proof of how good you are is if you play within the rules.

• Dad •

Billy and I both grew up to become baseball players like our dad, so a lot of people have talked about our father-son relationship. But actually, Dad was gone a lot of the time we were growing up.

He would be away on road trips, or scouting players across the country. Dad has said on many occasions that he spent more time with his players than he did with his own children.

It was hard on us, and hard on Dad too. He was afraid he was neglecting us at times. But I never felt that way. He was always *there* in the way that counts.

I just remember missing him sometimes. That's why I spend as much time as possible with my own kids, and that's why I can't see myself as a manager after I retire as a player. You don't see your family enough.

When Dad was home, it was great. The entire family played a lot of three-on-three basketball, even Mom. She had played on her high school team, and had a really good two-handed set shot.

Our big meal of the day was early in the afternoon, usually steaks on the grill. Dad would always say, "Drink your milk, Cal," something he repeated years later when the two of us did some radio commercials.

For all our meals at home Dad enforced a strict dress code—clean hands, clean shirt, combed hair. On the rare occasions we went out to a restaurant, he frowned on blue jeans. Sometimes Elly had to wear a dress. We even had a dress code for bowling and ball games. When I got to the majors, I drove Dad crazy by flipping up the bill of my cap like an inside-out umbrella.

There isn't a lot of money in minor league baseball today, and there was even less when I was growing up. Dad did what he had to do to support the family. Over the winters he managed a pharmacy, drove a delivery truck, worked at a hardware store and a lumberyard. He was usually out the door at dawn and asleep on the couch after supper, dog-tired.

• Mom •

The fact is, my *mom* was both mother and father a lot of the time.

While Dad was away, it was Mom who came to my father-son events. She was always at my Little League games, sitting in a lawn chair along the third-base line so that she wouldn't have to hear the parents in the bleachers yelling at their kids. She was the one who was keeping score, telling me to keep my eye on the ball, and patting me on the back whether I'd won or lost.

We didn't think about it at the time, but it must have been rough on her—all that packing and unpacking, living all over the country, pregnancies and babies and arguing kids. My mother says now that she'd pity anyone living today the way we did. But at the time, those were the facts of life. She didn't feel it was a "negative" situation. It was just the way things were. You went about your business and got the job done.

Those childhood years stand out in my memory. Elly, Fred, Billy, and I understood that we didn't live like most families. Moving around so much was tough on all of us, but there are a lot worse ways to grow up, I know now.

Today, we Ripkens remain a close family, and we still manage to get together a few times a year. I might not talk with Elly or Fred for months. But when one of us picks up the phone, it's as if we had talked yesterday. Maybe we spent so much time together growing up, and were so dependent on each other for friendship, that now this closeness is taken for granted.

• Be Like Dad •

You may have heard the expression "The apple doesn't fall far from the tree." It means a kid usually ends up to be a lot like his parents. I've always,

8

sometimes without even knowing it, patterned my life after my dad, Cal Ripken, Sr.

He was a hard worker who loved his work. On the ball field he often told his players, "Practice doesn't make perfect. Perfect practice makes perfect."

Before each season he always took us kids to an abandoned high school gym to pitch to us and get his arm in shape for throwing batting practice. He'd hit us hundreds of sharp grounders on the hardwood floors. When a ball nailed one of the kids on the shin, Dad would tell us to shake it off.

"The ball only weighs five and a quarter ounces," he would tease. We heard this *all* the time.

Dad could do anything—pitch, catch, smooth out the infield, drive the team bus, *fix* the bus if it broke down, even pour concrete for the dugouts. He used to carry tools in his back pocket so that he could repair any machine.

He was tough. Every winter he would take it upon himself to plow the roads and driveways around our house after heavy snowfalls. For this he used an old wooden plow towed by a tractor.

Once he took me and Fred to the barn and showed us how to crank the tractor engine. If you did it the wrong way, Dad explained, the engine could backfire and throw the crank off. He proceeded to demonstrate, and sure enough the engine backfired. The crank flew off and cracked him right on the forehead. Blood spurted out.

Dad reached for a greasy rag. I was sure we were

going to go to the hospital. But Dad just went into the house and put on some butterfly bandages. Then he got the tractor started and plowed the neighborhood streets as if nothing had happened.

Dad could be hardheaded, and I guess I inherited quite a bit of this feature. I think that some of my baseball behavior must have been an effort to prove to myself or to him that I'm a "gamer" too.

I realize that the man I've been describing here sounds like a rough, gruff guy—the kind of guy who might have pushed his sons to follow in his baseball footsteps. But Dad wasn't that way at all. He would have been the last person in the world to try to pressure Elly, Fred, Billy, or me into living our lives according to his plan. One of his strongest beliefs is that you should do what you enjoy.

Dad always said, "Be yourself and prove yourself." The pressure he *did* put on us was this: Whatever we do in life, we should do correctly and to the best of our abilities. He hates anything shoddy or lazy.

One day not long ago my own children, Rachel and Ryan, were arguing over something. I heard Rachel tell Ryan, "You're just trying to be like Daddy."

I turned to Rachel and said, "What's wrong with being like Dad? After all, that's what I've always tried to do."

2 · Teenage Years

If my dad never pushed baseball on me, then how did I fall in love with the game? It happened little by little.

When I was nine years old and Dad was managing the Rochester Red Wings (a Triple-A team in the Baltimore Orioles organization), I shared a bedroom with my brothers, Fred and Billy. On Saturday mornings Dad would peek his head in and ask who wanted to go with him to a clinic he gave to Little Leaguers and their coaches.

Fred was never interested. Billy was too young. Girls didn't play Little League back then, so Elly wasn't invited even though she was a great athlete.

I went along. But I didn't go for the baseball. The clinics were boring to me. I went along because it was my chance to have Dad all to myself for a little while. I knew he enjoyed having me along too.

The next year I joined Dad on two road trips. We were together all the time, and I got to wear a Red Wings uniform. I felt really grown-up, riding in airplanes and being away from home for the first time.

Over the next few summers, as we got older, all the Ripken kids would help out at the ballpark. We would sell candy, mop the clubhouse, do anything that needed to be done. Elly swept the bases after the fifth inning, occasionally giving the umpire a whack on the butt or a kiss on the cheek.

Sometimes Dad let me hit a few balls and field some grounders before the players arrived. I wasn't allowed on the infield dirt because we didn't want to scuff it up. But every so often I would put on Dad's old catching gear and get behind the plate for some throws from the batting practice pitcher—Dad. These were the hardest pitches I'd ever seen.

Little by little baseball became more than just a way to hang out with my dad. I really enjoyed it, and I was getting good at it. Plus, I noticed that the Double-A players I saw over those summers— some of them just five or six years older than me— were having a blast. I began to think about a career in pro ball. Ever since then I've never thought about doing anything else.

I tried to soak up everything I could. I pestered the players for tips, questioning them about the smallest details I observed.

At home I played hundreds of games against Fred, Elly, Billy, or myself if necessary. The great Oriole third baseman Brooks Robinson was my hero, and when I made a great backyard stab, I would yell his name. Billy was younger than me, so when we played, I only got one out at the plate and I had to play left-handed in the field.

We were living in Asheville, North Carolina, during those summers. They had a great Little League program, with good fields and coaches. I think those summers were really important to my development as a player.

One year we won the state championship. The whole team went door-to-door to collect money, and we raised enough for a trip to Florida for the southeastern regionals. We didn't make it to the Little League World Series, but we did pretty well. We won the first game in Florida, but lost the second one.

I was pitching, and I gave up the key homer. It was a high fly that barely cleared the left field fence. I wanted to blame our fielder for not reaching over and catching the ball, but ended up blaming myself for throwing the pitch in the first place. I was crying along with everyone else.

• High School •

After three summers in Asheville, our traveling days were finally over in 1975. Dad became a scout for the Orioles, based in Baltimore.

As a high school freshman that year, I made the varsity baseball team—because they needed a second baseman. I was just fourteen, and weighed about 125 pounds.

I got four hits in about thirty-five at bats that season. Playing against all those juniors and seniors, I was overmatched. The coach asked me to bunt a lot.

One time there was a slow bouncer to shortstop. The runner at first, a huge kid named Steve Slagle, came barreling toward second. He was on the football team, and he loved contact. I stretched for the throw with my back to the runner and Slagle flattened me.

I don't remember what happened next very well because I was on my back with the breath knocked out of me. But I was told that I begged, "Don't take me out, Coach, I'm okay!"

While I was on the boys' varsity, Elly was the star of the girls' varsity softball team. They played in the opposite corner of a big field, and there was no outfield fence for either diamond. When a ball from the girls' game rolled onto our field, it was usually one of Elly's homers.

Elly was a terrific athlete. She received varsity letters in basketball, volleyball, and softball all four years in high school. I was immature physically, and shy and introverted socially. My teammates used to kid me that my sister was better than me. Elly's teammates teased me and pinched my cheek all the time, making me blush violently.

At some point I quit walking home from school with Elly. This hurt her feelings, but it was just too embarrassing.

Toward the end of the season Dad took me into a batting cage and worked with me to improve my bat speed. I'd been waiting until the ball was thrown before I started my swing. I could get away with that in Little League, but high school pitchers threw much harder.

In just one session Dad taught me to turn in my left shoulder during the pitcher's windup. In my next at bat I stroked a line drive up the middle. Then I lined out to center field. Those were the two hardest hit balls I'd had all year.

During my sophomore and junior years, I got much better. I played on a sixteen-and-younger league in the summer. Dad was coaching for the Orioles by that time, and my games usually took place at the same time as his. He didn't have much of a chance to see me play.

I know I cared about his absence, because when he *was* able to be there, I tried too hard and didn't play well. I only struck out four times my whole senior year, but three of them were in one of the few games Dad could attend.

I used to drive over to Memorial Stadium, where the Orioles played in those days, to pick up Dad after his games. Waiting for him in the clubhouse,

I'd talk with Doug DeCinces, Kenny Singleton, Mark Belanger, and Eddie Murray.

By that time I was really into baseball. *Totally* into baseball. Driving home, I'd pepper Dad with questions. I was beginning to understand how to analyze a game and how to think like a player.

One day I cleared the fence at Memorial Stadium off one of my dad's batting practice pitches. He was beginning to take me seriously as a ballplayer.

• Other Challenges •

The funny thing is, Dad really knew me more as a soccer player than a baseball player back then. He loves the game, and he coached two or three teams each winter. While we were growing up, all the Ripken kids played soccer.

In high school, I was also a pretty good basketball player, but I gave it up after one season. I made up a lot of excuses, but the real reason is I was kind of a late bloomer.

I had no hair on my chest or underarms.

It's true. I was embarrassed to wear the uniform. It was even worse if I was on the "skins" team in practice. As I mentioned, I matured late physically, and I was a typically awkward teenager. Just look at the picture of me on my way to the senior prom!

I was a good student, though. Math was my best subject. For me, the great thing about math was that there was always a right answer.

In algebra I had a really good teacher who liked to challenge us with a tough homework problem every night. Most days this one girl in the class was the only student to get it right. Then one day the class was given a problem that our teacher said was *really* hard.

I guess I had less homework than usual that night, and I accepted the challenge. I worked for hours on the problem, really grinding. Finally, at one o'clock in the morning, I figured it out. I wanted to shout, but the whole family was asleep.

The next day at school the teacher asked if anyone had been able to solve the problem. I looked over at the girl. She didn't raise her hand. I raised mine, and was called to the blackboard to show my work.

My equations took the entire front blackboard and part of the smaller one. When I finished and the teacher told me I was right, I felt great.

• Decision Time •

Senior year was decision time. I was a good student and could have gone on to college. But I had an all-consuming drive to play major league baseball. After thinking it over for a long time, I decided to go with baseball.

I had shot up—to six feet two and 185 pounds—during high school. Scouts from the majors started coming to my games when I was a junior.

I was mostly a pitcher then. I had a good fastball—eighty-seven miles per hour—a very good curve, a slider, and a pretty effective change-up. And I had command of those pitches. During senior year, my record was 7-2 with a .79 ERA. But I also played a good shortstop, hitting .496 and leading the team in hits and RBIs.

I didn't care what position I played, as long as a major league team drafted me. I wanted to be an everyday player, like a shortstop, but most teams were interested in me as a pitcher. Dad said that if I started as a shortstop but didn't make the grade, I could go back after a couple of years and try to be a pitcher. It would be much more difficult to start as a pitcher and then try to move to shortstop.

I preferred playing short too, but for a different reason. I liked the action. I wanted to be in the lineup. Pitching is great when you're on the mound. You're in total control, and there's no better feeling. But after the game, you have to wait four days for your next start. What would I do for four days?

Even back then I knew I wanted to play every day.

Deep inside, I hoped my dad's team—the Orioles—would pick me in the annual baseball draft. But any team would have been fine. With trades and everything, you never know where you're going to end up anyway.

I went to school on the morning of the baseball draft like it was any other day. I don't remember all of the details, but I think somebody from the office gave me the news that the Baltimore Orioles had drafted me. I was their third pick of the second round, the forty-eighth selection overall.

There wasn't any big celebration in the Ripken house that night. Dad conveyed his pride with a handshake, a look, and a certain pat on the back. That meant more to me than any celebration.

My dream had come true. I was going to the pros!

3 · The Minors

Maybe some people think baseball players go directly from high school to being stars in the major leagues. Far from it! Most of us spent at least three years in the minors. I did. It was frustrating at times, fun at others, and a real learning experience all around.

I was assigned to play shortstop for the Bluefield Orioles, a team in Bluefield, West Virginia. I'll never forget my first game in Rookie League. Opening Day, 1978, in Paintsville, Kentucky, against the Highlanders. I was seventeen years old, barely shaving. I had never been away from my family for any length of time.

Conditions on Opening Day at the Highlanders' home field were not exactly major league. In their bullpen, there were weeds up to the knees of the relief pitchers, I recall.

Hardly any fans showed up that day. That was lucky, because I made three errors. I wasn't much better at the plate.

I had been a star player back home in Maryland, but that didn't help me in Rookie League. I didn't fare too well in the beginning. There were guys who had college experience, guys who were mature players. Those first two or three weeks were a low point.

Some people may have thought I had only been drafted because my dad was a coach for the Orioles.

I never thought about calling it quits—no way. My plan was to give professional baseball five or six years. If I didn't make it after that, I'd enroll in college.

In the meantime there were a lot of long distance phone calls home for reassurance. Dad usually had the same advice: Get back to basics.

Things picked up a little as the season went on. My hitting improved, and I ended up with a respectable .264 average. No homers, though. Dad assured me that power comes with waiting on the ball, and most young hitters have trouble waiting.

My fielding statistics weren't too great. I made thirty-two errors in sixty-three games, sometimes throwing the ball into the stands.

That season I lived with three other young players in a boardinghouse run by an elderly lady named Mrs. Short. She cooked our meals and did our laundry for us. She couldn't come to our games because of her arthritis, but sometimes she and her dog would join us on the front porch to talk about the game when we got back.

For the cooking, cleaning, and companionship, Mrs. Short charged us just twenty-five dollars a week. I was getting paid one hundred dollars a week, so I actually saved some money that season.

We were fairly well behaved at Mrs. Short's, for a bunch of teenagers. It was a different story on road trips. On the last day of the trips, the whole team was often packed into two or three motel rooms from noon until we left for the game at 5:00 P.M., to save money.

These crowded conditions led to some all-out wrestling matches. I love to wrestle, and sometimes things got out of hand. We messed up a few of those motel rooms and destroyed some luggage, I have to admit.

But mostly, we spent our time talking about baseball. All of us had the same desire to make the majors. When we weren't playing baseball, we read about it or watched it on TV. We ate, drank, and slept baseball.

After the short Rookie League season, the Orioles invited me to Instructional League in St. Petersburg, Florida. That was a good sign. Players don't get invited unless somebody sees potential in them.

I played every inning of every game in Instructional League. My fielding improved and something started clicking for me at the plate. I actually hit a few homers.

I began keeping notes on all the pitchers we were facing and their pitch sequences. I kept this up in St. Pete. Nobody else on the team did this, and I was a little embarrassed about it, so I didn't tell the other guys. I ended up keeping notes on pitchers the whole time I was in the minors. I kept doing it in the majors too, and didn't stop until the coaching staff started tracking the same information for all the players.

The best part of Instructional League was when Dad came to visit for a couple of weeks. We spent more time together than we ever did before. Something odd occurred to me—if I eventually made it to the Orioles, the game that took my father away so much when I was a kid would bring us together as adults.

A hitter's bat is obviously crucial. Hitters are always searching for their perfect bat. In high school I used my dad's old bats that I found in the attic. In Rookie League I swung a Louisville Slugger M-110. But when I was moved up to the Orioles A-ball Miami team in 1979, I received a shipment of M-159s by mistake.

The length and weight of the two bats were the same (thirty-five inches, thirty-two ounces), but the M-159s had a skinnier handle and more weight in the barrel. The bat felt whippier, and it felt good.

The same night I got my new bats, with the game scoreless in the twelfth inning, I slammed my first official minor league homer. The crowd would have gone wild—if there had been a crowd. It was late and they had gone home.

I had found my perfect bat. I used that same type model through my major league career, switching to the similar P-72, and adding one ounce as I got stronger.

• Getting Confidence •

I did well in A-ball, and was moved over to third base when the regular third baseman got hurt. I was comfortable there right away. Ground balls get to you quicker at third than they do at short-stop. That gives you more time to stop the ball, set yourself, and throw.

The next season (1980) I played third base every game when I was promoted to the Orioles Double-A team in Charlotte, North Carolina.

That was a breakthrough season for me. I had been putting on five pounds every year, and I was close to two hundred pounds. I had grown to six feet three inches. I was getting stronger, and it showed in my hitting. A strong guy can hit a ball off the handle of the bat and still muscle it over the infield for a hit. Weaker hitters can't do that.

That's one advantage strength gives a hitter. The other, of course, is that when a stronger guy hits the ball with the sweet spot of the bat, it has a bet-ter chance of going over the wall. I hit twenty-five homers in Double-A ball, with seventy-eight RBIs.

I was becoming a smarter player too. At the plate

I was confident enough to start looking for pitches from certain pitchers in certain situations. I began to study the opposing hitters too. If you know a guy can get around on one pitch or has trouble with another one, it helps you know where to position yourself in the field.

The clubhouse was funky and half the showers never worked, but my season at Charlotte was the best year I had in the minors, and one of my most enjoyable in baseball. We won the Southern League championship, and I was starting to come into my own.

• The Strangest Game •

I had played six hundred games in three years. That was the way I wanted it. Playing was learning. I was burning to get into the big leagues, and that was the way to do it. I felt I was closing in. Things looked good. *Really* good.

And then I got hurt.

It happened just after I had been sent down from Big League camp to join the Orioles' Triple-A team, the Rochester Red Wings, in spring training. I took a swing in the batting cage and pulled something in my right shoulder. It hurt badly.

I had missed a few games in Rookie League and A-ball because of a sore shoulder, but *this* felt like a serious injury.

What bad timing! I was one step away from the majors. This was the first real injury of my career—

and it could have been the last. In many cases a simple sore arm *ends* a player's career.

The trainers forbade me to throw or hit. All I could do was run. That was my whole day. It drove me crazy.

There was talk of putting me on the disabled list, but my shoulder started feeling better and I talked the manager into letting me test it. I hit the ball pretty well in batting practice, with no pain.

They let me into a few games and I got lucky. I didn't hit the ball hard, but every grounder I hit seemed to find a hole. I was allowed to start the season with the rest of the team, and the shoulder never bothered me again.

I played in one of the strangest games in baseball history that season. It was in Pawtucket, Rhode Island. The temperature was nearly freezing and the wind was blowing straight in. Everybody hoped we could get the game over with quickly.

We had the lead, but Pawtucket tied it up in the bottom of the ninth inning. We would have to play extra innings. A *lot* of extra innings.

Neither team could score through the tenth, the fifteenth, even the twentieth inning! We managed to push a run across the plate in the twenty-first, and everybody thought the game was over. But Pawtucket tied it up again.

We were so cold, somebody got an empty oil drum and built a fire in it right in the dugout.

Unbelievably, the game reached the thirtieth inning, and it was *still* tied! We almost scored in

26

the thirty-second, but our runner got thrown out at the plate.

By that time we had played for *eight* hours. The umpires decided to stop the game at that point. We all went home, exhausted, and tried to get some sleep.

Two months later the two teams picked up where we'd left off in the thirty-second inning. This time there were TV crews from all over to record the historic event.

Pawtucket ended up winning the game on a single in the bottom of the thirty-third inning. The game was finally over! I went 2-for-13 for the game, by the way.

Other than that long, strange game, it was a great year. I hit a homer on my third at bat of the season. Later in the summer I got red-hot, hitting three homers in one game.

On August 8, our manager, Doc Edwards, called me into his office. I had been called up to join the Baltimore Orioles!

4 · The Rookie

If you think that once you reach the big leagues you've got it made, you've got it wrong.

The Orioles didn't have a permanent place for me to play when they called me up at the end of the 1981 season. The shortstop and third baseman, Mark Belanger and Doug DeCinces, were solid veterans. The team was in a pennant race, so Manager Earl Weaver wasn't about to trust a rookie in pressure situations.

My first big league appearance was being called in to pinch-run in the twelfth inning of a game against Kansas City. It was incredibly exciting for me. Here I was, not yet twenty-one, and living every kid's fantasy—playing in the big leagues.

The KC second baseman, Frank White, tried to pick me off right away. I scurried back to the bag safely and White said, "Just checking, kid."

I didn't see much action that year. I ended the season with only thirty-nine big-league at bats. Five hits. No homers. No RBIs.

My confidence got sort of beaten down. I thought I might have been better off playing every day in the minors than sitting on a major league bench chewing sunflower seeds. That's when I started thinking that if I ever broke into the regular line-up, I would play every day.

After the season was over, I caught a break. While I was playing winter ball in Puerto Rico, the Orioles traded Doug DeCinces. I had known Doug ever since I was a kid hanging around the Oriole club-house. He was a great guy and a good friend to me. But I also knew the trade opened up a huge opportunity. With Doug traded, third base would be mine to lose in 1982.

• The Slump •

My "official" rookie season started off with a bang. I hit a homer in my first at bat and went 3-for-5 on Opening Day.

Then I went into a deep, deep slump.

A slump is like when you have a bad day, every day, for a long time. I just couldn't hit the ball, and I didn't know why.

I was always very patient at the plate. I usually wouldn't swing at the first pitch, because I wanted to get a look at what the pitcher was throwing. But in the big leagues, pitchers caught on to that, and they started throwing me first-pitch fastballs down the middle of the plate. Strike one.

I was behind in the count right away. Then came a slider for strike two. A two-strike count is a big disadvantage for even the best hitters. I usually ended up with a strikeout or a weak grounder.

The slump got worse and worse. Pitchers were constantly throwing me fastballs while I was looking for curves. They busted me inside while I was guessing they would aim for the outside corner. I was overanalyzing and overwhelmed. I just couldn't hit the ball.

Everybody tried to help. Dad kept telling me to get back to basics. We experimented by having me move closer to the plate. Earl Weaver kept assuring me he wasn't going to send me back to the minors. But I was afraid he was losing patience.

I tried everything except playing video games to improve my eye-hand coordination (that's what my teammate Eddie Murray did). Nothing worked. I couldn't even get a hit off my dad during batting practice, which I'd been doing since I was a teenager. At one point I had four hits in fifty-five at bats.

On May 1 we were playing the Angels, and the great Reggie Jackson was the runner on third base. "Look, don't let everyone else tell you how to hit," Reggie advised me. "You could hit before you got here. Just be yourself and hit the way you want to hit. They traded DeCinces to make room for you, didn't they? They think you can play. They *know* you can."

Other people had been giving me basically the

same advice—quit worrying so much, play my best, let the chips fall where they may. But somehow, coming from a slugger who would end up with 563 homers, the words finally sank in.

I got two hits the next day (which brought my average *up* to .141!). After the second hit I glanced in the Angels dugout and saw Reggie nodding and laughing. My slump was over and I felt great.

• A Mission •

Sometimes, just when you get on your feet, something comes along and knocks you down. In my case it was a baseball.

It was the fifth inning, the day after I broke out of my slump. I was facing Mike Moore, a hard-throwing rookie. Moore had already gotten me to hit a weak come-backer off his breaking ball. I was looking for another one. Pitchers usually keep throwing you the same pitch until you prove you can hit it.

The pitch came in and I tried to pick up the spin. I waited for the ball to break. And I waited. And I waited. Then, I suddenly realized the ball wasn't going to break. I had guessed wrong. It wasn't a breaking ball. It was a ninety-four-mile-per-hour heater.

It clocked me right in the back of the head.

I was flat on my back. There was a dent and a crack in my batting helmet. I was sent to the hospital as a precaution, but I was okay.

When a hitter comes back after getting beaned,

everybody watches him closely. Does he look more determined? Or does he look like he's afraid of the ball? If word gets around that you can be intimidated by high inside pitches, naturally you're going to see a lot of high inside pitches.

When I came back, I was on a mission to prove I couldn't be intimidated. The beaning had woken me up. It made me more determined. By the time we came back from a West Coast road trip, my average had gone up ninety points.

In the middle of all this, on May 29, Earl Weaver sat me down for the second game of a doubleheader. It wasn't a big deal at the time, but it would be later. That was the last game I would miss for the next sixteen years.

• The Switch •

The other important thing that happened during my rookie season took place on July 1. I walked into the clubhouse before the game that day and saw my name on the lineup card—in the shortstop position.

Earl Weaver had thought of me as a shortstop ever since he saw me fielding grounders when I was a teenager. After my hitting came around, he decided to switch me from third to short. I knew the basics about playing the position, but I hadn't played there for several years.

Earl told me to just make the routine plays and not worry about the fancy stuff. At first it was almost like learning the game all over again. But little by little, I felt more comfortable at short. Every time a new play came up that I handled, I told myself, *Okay, that's one more you know you can make.* Slowly my confidence grew until I could make all the plays.

• So Close •

The Orioles' season sort of mirrored my own. Early on, we lost sixteen out of twenty-three games. It looked as if it was all over for us. But then we got hot and won seventeen out of eighteen.

Going into the last weekend of the season, we were three games behind the Milwaukee Brewers with four games left to play. We had to win all four games to win the division. It was a long shot.

We were playing at home, and the energy in the stands that weekend was incredible. Earl Weaver had announced his retirement a few weeks earlier, so we really wanted to win the pennant for him.

We won the first game, and we were feeling pretty good. When we won the second game, we felt the momentum going our way. Then we stomped the Brewers 11-3 in the third game, and the crowd went absolutely crazy.

We were tied for first place with the Brewers. Whichever team won the final game of the season would win the division.

It was a classic pitching matchup between two Hall of Famers—Jim Palmer for the Orioles and

Don Sutton for the Brewers. Baltimore fans in the stands were waving brooms. They desperately wanted us to sweep the series.

It didn't happen. Robin Yount hit two homers for the Brewers and they beat us. We finished in second place.

There were a number of great rookies in the American League my first full season: Kent Hrbek, Wade Boggs, Von Hayes, Tom Brunansky, Gary Gaetti. I had put up good numbers—a respectable .264 average, with a quite respectable twenty-eight home runs and ninety-three RBIs—but any of those guys could have been a deserving Rookie of the Year.

The night the vote was to be announced, at about eleven o'clock, the phone rang. It was Jack Lang, executive director of the Baseball Writers Association of America. He only had to say one word—"Congratulations." I had been named Rookie of the Year.

• Old Friends •

It had been an incredible year. When it was all said and done, the only thing I felt bad about was that a lot of my buddies I'd played with in the minors hadn't made it to the big leagues. A lot of them never would.

The friendships you make in the minors are often closer than those you have at the major league level. When a group of guys shares those long bus rides, those bumpy ballfields in the middle of nowhere, the crummy food, and the lack of money, you can't help but become close. We relied on each other for everything. A lot of guys say their time in the minors was the most fun they had in baseball.

You may never have heard the names Will George, Tim Norris, or Brooks Carey. But they were just a few of the talented players who were my friends in the minor leagues. When it became clear that he wouldn't make the big leagues, Will became a scout. Tim works for a printing company today. Brooks runs the family auto parts business.

From the start, we all knew that the odds were against us. Only two out of every one hundred guys who sign professional contracts actually play a big league game. Still, everybody plays their heart out in an effort to be one of those two guys.

I remember that when we were two struggling bushers dreaming of the majors, Brooks Carey used to say to me, "I just want to get up there for one game."

I wish Brooks's dream had come true like mine did.

5 · *1983*

I have a reputation for being a sort of serious, no-nonsense guy both on and off the field. Well, now the truth can be told! The Oriole teams I played on from 1982 to 1986 were a pretty loose bunch of guys, and I had as much fun as anyone else.

I roomed with our catcher Rick Dempsey on road trips back then. Rick had an uncanny knack for getting duplicate hotel room keys. After we snuck inside somebody's room, we would booby-trap the place.

Our favorite target was Tom Marr, one of the Orioles' broadcasters. Rick and I terrorized the poor guy. We rigged a bucket over Tom's door so that when he opened it, water would fall on his head. We glued his toiletries to the counter in the bathroom. We stretched plastic wrap across his toilet bowl (an old trick, but it still works). We stuffed pine needles and pine cones in his bed.

Once, in the middle of the night, Rick and I armed ourselves with fire extinguishers and knocked on Tom's door. When he groggily peered out, we opened fire, filling the room with foam.

Ah, those were the days!

I settled down somewhat over the years. Part of the reason was that I got married and had kids. There was simply less time for fooling around with the guys. The other part was that I became more conscious of the relationship between Cal Ripken the baseball player and Cal Ripken the person.

Whether I liked it or not, my actions, I came to realize, influenced kids. Just as I had looked up to athletes when I was a boy, some kids were now looking up to me.

I'm sure you've seen players in all sports get frustrated and throw tantrums on the field. When I was a young player, it always impressed me the way real pros like Eddie Murray, Frank Robinson, and Brooks Robinson would calmly return their helmet and bat to the dugout after an embarrassing at bat. They might have let off some steam in private, but they didn't put on public tantrums.

I decided early on that I wanted to be that kind of player. Baseball can be very frustrating, and there are times when you boil over. But I feel a player also has a responsibility to the fans and to his team. After you've been ejected from a game, you can't do any good for anybody that day.

I'm not perfect. I've had some episodes I wish I could take back. Once I was thrown out of a game in the first inning after arguing that a called strike was off the plate. That night I was told that a boy and his father had driven from Virginia just to see me play. The boy spent the last eight innings of the game in tears. That really bothered me, and it stuck with me.

• Some Year! •

As I said, the Orioles were a loose, happy team. Maybe that's why we just *rolled* from the first day of spring training in 1983. We easily won the American League East title, and then beat the White Sox to win the pennant. In that series our pitching staff only gave up three runs in four games.

I didn't start the year with a big slump, as I did my rookie year. I put up some good, solid numbers and made the All-Star team for the first time. In the second half of the season I really caught fire, hitting about .340 for almost three months. The hits came in bunches.

Playing in the World Series was a lifetime fantasy I got to fulfill. The TV, radio, and newspaper people whipped up a lot of excitement, scrutinizing every play. But I was surprised how relaxed I became after the first ground ball came my way. *That was just like a grounder in July,* I remember thinking to myself.

Like anyone else, players fall back on what we know and how we've been trained. Even when it is the World Series, baseball becomes baseball, and you lose yourself in the game.

The Philadelphia Phillies had won the National League pennant. They beat us in Game 1 of the World Series. But then we stormed back and won four in a row, the last three in Philadelphia. When I caught the humpbacked liner from Garry Maddox for the final out of the Series, the celebration began.

I'd heard for years that *getting* to the World Series is more exciting than winning it. I found there was some truth to that. But it still felt great to win.

• Eddie Murray •

After the Series was over, people started talking about who deserved to win the American League's Most Valuable Player Award. My name came up, along with Eddie Murray, and Jim Rice of the Boston Red Sox. Eddie and I never talked about it.

We had almost identical statistics, but I thought Eddie was the most valuable player to our team. A lot of my success was due to him.

You see, I hit number three in the batting order with Eddie right behind me in the cleanup position. Pitchers knew Eddie was the best clutch hitter in the game (he hit about .400 with runners in scoring position), so they didn't want to risk walking me and facing Eddie. I got good pitches to hit all year.

Eddie was not only one of the best players I ever

played with, he was also one of the best guys I ever knew. He was always throwing crab feasts at his house, and every September he would invite the rookies to stay at his house if they needed a place to live.

When I reached the majors, Eddie was already a star. During infield practice, after he'd taken his ground balls, he would come over and talk with me. He taught me how to think and behave like a big leaguer. How to relax. Keep things simple. Stay within yourself. Teammates come first. No false hustle. No complaints. That sort of thing.

Eddie never participated in the hotel room pranks Rick Dempsey and I used to pull. He told me that I put too much energy into goofing off, and I got the message. I was lucky to have a friend like him, and I'll always be grateful to him. I think he was the perfect teammate.

On a barnstorming tour of Japan one year, Eddie and I were sitting around looking at statistics. "You know, Big Ed," I told him, "you have the chance to hit five hundred home runs. You can get three thousand hits." I was surprised when Eddie said those numbers didn't mean anything to him. He said he was just going to do his best. He meant that too.

Most people don't know this, but my dad played a role in Eddie Murray's career. Eddie was playing for Asheville in the minors at the time. He was a right-handed hitter, but one day he took batting practice left-handed as a drill. He hit the ball pretty well, so naturally there was talk about turning him into a switch-hitter.

Some people in the Orioles organization didn't like the idea. They felt Eddie had great potential, and didn't want to mess things up by experimenting on him.

Dad was a scout that season. When he came through Asheville, he watched Eddie bat right- and left-handed. He didn't see any problem with Eddie as a switch-hitter, and he got permission from the front office for the experiment to continue.

The result, of course, was that Eddie went on to become one of the greatest switch-hitters in baseball history.

Anyway, Eddie and I both had great seasons in 1983. If I won the MVP, I'd be thrilled. If Eddie won, I'd also be thrilled. He had finished second in the voting in 1982, and I felt he deserved it.

As it turned out, I got 322 votes and Eddie got 290, probably because many people consider the shortstop position more crucial to a team's defense than first base. But whatever the case, I was the American League's Most Valuable Player!

I called Mom and Dad as soon as I got the news, and they drove over to celebrate with me. The next day Eddie called to congratulate me.

What a way to begin a career! In my first two years the Orioles had just missed winning our division and then won the World Series. For myself, I'd won Rookie of the Year and then MVP. I felt I had arrived as a big leaguer.

6 · Three Ripkens

When a team wins the World Series, a lot of people expect them to repeat the next season. In reality, the team that wins the Series hardly *ever* repeats.

The 1984 season was a disappointment. Our pitching held up, but we didn't score runs when we needed them. We dropped from scoring 799 runs to 681. That's a big dip. Some guys were hurt, others had a bad year.

Another problem was that the Detroit Tigers won twelve of their first thirteen games and thirty-five of their first forty. It's almost impossible to catch a team that starts off that hot. We ended up winning eighty-five games, but finished in fifth place.

My personal highlight of 1984 was playing in the All-Star game with my father as the batting practice pitcher. It was the first father-son combo in All-Star history.

The next year it was our pitchers' turn to struggle. Our ace, Jim Palmer, had retired. The remaining starters slipped. In June 1985 Joe Altobelli was fired as manager.

We were a team in transition. My dad was temporary manager for one game (which he won), and then Earl Weaver was brought out of retirement to run the club. For a brief moment I thought Earl was going to work his magic one more time. But then a bunch of guys got hurt and we finished fourth.

Things got worse in 1986. The Orioles had their first losing season since I was seven years old. Twelve guys went on the disabled list, including Eddie Murray.

We just couldn't catch a break. In one game we hit two grand-slam home runs in a single inning— and we *still* lost!

As a team we committed a club record 135 errors. We lost our focus and concentration. We staggered to the end of the season by losing forty-two games while we won just fourteen. Dead last in the American League East.

The newspapers said we quit, but that wasn't true. All we could do was look forward to next year.

• A New Manager •

When Earl Weaver announced he wouldn't be returning to manage the Orioles for 1987, the guessing games began. Would pitching coach

Ray Miller get the job? Or maybe it would be Oriole legend Frank Robinson? And there was one other loyal Oriole man who was qualified— Cal Ripken, Sr.

My dad had been working in the Baltimore organization as a coach, scout, or minor league manager for thirty years. His name had come up several times before when the manager's job was open, but he never got the job.

Some people said the Orioles might hire Dad as manager because he had worked so long for the team, and because the team "owed" him. Others said Dad might be given the job to keep me on the team when my contract expired.

People seemed to consider a lot of reasons, but the insiders knew the three obvious reasons: Dad had the experience. The players respected him. He was qualified.

The day he got the news that he would be the next manager of the Baltimore Orioles, there might even have been some tears shed by the seemingly unsentimental Ripken family.

It was going to be great playing under my dad.

One day in my rookie season when Dad was our third-base coach, I had made the mistake of calling him "Dad" in front of my teammates. Instantly, all the guys were making fun of me, running around saying, "Dad! Oh, *Dad!*" After that, I always called my dad "Senior" or "Number 47."

• A New Teammate •

What added to that season was that the Orioles had a hot new second baseman in the spring of 1987—Billy Ripken.

My kid brother, whom I had terrorized all through our younger years, had grown up to be a fine ballplayer. After being drafted by the Orioles in the eleventh round in 1982, Billy worked his way through the minors and earned a shot at the big leagues.

There had been plenty of brother combinations in baseball history before Billy and me, but this was to be the first time brothers would be managed by their *father*.

A reporter asked Billy if he and I had ever played baseball on the same team before. I was surprised to realize that the answer was no. We had played hundreds of pickup games as kids, but we had never even played in the same *league* before.

As kids, the four-year age difference between us made it seem like we were from different generations. But as two adults, the age difference didn't seem so big anymore.

My brother and I are very similar in some ways, and very different in other ways. We're both competitive, which led to the feuds we had growing up. When the two of us got together, things would often "get simple," as Dad put it.

Billy refused to accept the huge disadvantage he

faced in size and age. When I teased him, he'd blow his top. Once I drove him berserk by squirting him with a water pistol through the screened top half of a locked door. He punched out the glass panel underneath and cut his arm pretty badly.

But Billy has a funny side too. He's much more of a class clown than I am. When he walks in the room, I smile. When he starts talking, I usually start laughing. Someone asked Dad if he called his son "Bill" or "Billy." Dad replied, "I call him motormouth."

In neighborhood games my little brother and I were a powerful combination. If I was picking one of the squads in a game, I'd choose Billy first. I guess I was looking out for him, but I also knew the other team might disregard him because he was much younger. Because of this, I threw plenty of touchdown passes to Billy. On the basketball court when I picked off an offensive rebound, I'd flip it to Bill for the open shot.

When I was in the minors, guys poked fun at me for being the son of Cal Ripken, Sr. For Billy, it was even *worse* being Dad's son and my little brother. He struggled in the beginning, just like me. He was smaller and thinner than me, and more susceptible to injuries. Various broken fingers and knee and shoulder problems slowed his progress through the minors.

As a brother and as a teammate, I was happy to play alongside Billy on the Orioles. He had earned the opportunity. He was also a smart infielder who had great hands.

The news media saw the three Ripkens as a great human interest story, and reporters were all over us that spring. *Sports Illustrated* put us on the cover.

Naturally, the first question thrown at Dad was, "Will the family relationship have any bearing on the decisions you will make as manager?"

"No bearing whatsoever," Dad snapped. He meant it. Billy and I knew we would be treated like any of the other players. We were Dad's sons *off* the field.

On the first day of spring training Dad greeted Billy with the same handshake and "Welcome aboard" that he gave to everyone else. He warned Billy not to expect to play every day, and that he would be replaced by pinch hitters in certain situations.

As it turned out, Billy nailed a homer in his first week in the big leagues and hit .308 in fifty-eight games. When that first home run went over the wall, I was screaming the whole time Billy was jogging around the bases.

Billy provided a big spark for us after the All-Star break, but the team couldn't keep the blaze going. Our pitching wasn't there, giving up 226 homers during the season and an average of five runs a game. A lot of guys got injured again.

It had been great playing on the same team as my brother and father. But it wasn't so great losing ninety-five games and finishing sixth.

• The First Streak •

After a few years in the big leagues, someone noticed that I played every game each season. Usually guys sit out a game or two—or a couple of innings—every so often to rest, even if they're not hurt.

Around the same time some sharp-eyed statisticians began to notice that I even played every *inning* of every game. That was unheard of. Usually, when the score becomes lopsided, the starters take an early shower.

To me, playing nine innings of a baseball game was no big deal, regardless of what was on the scoreboard. Besides, I still had that old-school attitude that once I was in a big league lineup, I wasn't going to come out.

A lot of people seem to forget that ballplayers don't play *continuously*. We get off days during the season. From October through February we don't play at all. But when my team is out there on the field, I want to be with them.

The record for "most consecutive innings played" didn't even exist. When I reached 7,000 and then 8,000 consecutive innings, some researchers figured out that nobody had ever done that, so the record was mine.

For some reason consecutive inning and game streaks seem to unnerve a lot of people. Every time a player on a streak goes into even a mild slump, people start saying he needs a rest. As if he's too *tired* to hit.

That's always seemed like nonsense to me. When I feel sluggish, it doesn't make me feel *better* to sit on the bench. Sitting out one or two innings isn't going to restore my energy. In fact, I perk *up* when I trot onto the field. I just want to play, period.

The manager, of course, decides who plays and how much he plays. With my dad managing the Orioles in 1987, it was *his* job to decide how much or how little I would play. He was the boss. He could end my consecutive innings streak anytime he wanted to.

Toward the end of that season we were playing the Blue Jays at Exhibition Stadium in Toronto. Our pitchers had given up ten homers and we were getting beaten pretty badly. I was due up fourth in our half of the eighth inning.

As I was getting ready to step out to the on-deck circle, Dad called me over and said very quietly, "What do you think about coming out?"

Dad and I had never discussed my consecutive innings streak up until that point. Not once.

"What do *you* think?" I asked him.

"I think it's a good idea," he replied.

"Okay."

With that simple exchange, my streak of playing 8,243 consecutive innings came to an end. That record still stands today.

If I had told Dad I wanted to stay in the game,

he would have left me in. But I had faith in his judgment. This one time he was dealing with me as my manager *and* as my father.

When my brother Billy realized what was going on, I thought he was going to cry. Seeing him made *me* feel like crying.

I had never put much stock in the consecutive innings streak as a *streak* to begin with. I just wanted to play ball every inning. But now that it was over, all of a sudden I could hardly breathe. I found myself overcome with emotion.

I stood in the runway behind the dugout by myself for a minute. Then the guys crowded around to shake my hand, my father included. Some of the guys kidded me, offering advice on how to sit on the bench.

After the game Dad and I got grilled by the press. He explained that the decision to take me out of the game was entirely his (many old-school managers like Dad would take the heat off their players). He said that he didn't want me to have to deal with the hassles of the streak the following year, when I would be approaching 10,000 innings.

Afterward, Dad and I spoke privately. He told me that sitting down for an inning now and then would be a good thing for me and for the team.

I respected Dad's decision. I wasn't angry. But perhaps without even realizing it until the streak was over, I felt strongly about playing more con-

secutive innings than anyone in baseball history. I
felt bad that the streak was over. I felt I had lost
the fight, almost like I had let myself down, abandoned my ideals.

Years later my brother Billy told me he looked at
my face as I was sitting on the bench during the
ninth inning of that game. He said he knew right
then it would be a long time before I missed an
entire game.

7 · Kelly, Rachel, and Ryan

One night I was eating dinner at a restaurant with my teammate Al Bumbry. An attractive lady came over to our table with her husband. The lady said her name was Joan Geer, and she asked for an autograph.

Before I started writing, Mrs. Geer told me, "Have I got a daughter for you!" She told me her daughter's name was Kelly.

I wrote on Mrs. Geer's napkin, "To Kelly, if you look anything like your mother, I'm sorry I missed you. Cal Ripken."

I don't know what came over me. It's not like me to make such a forward statement. But I'm glad I did. Four years later Joan Geer became my mother-in-law, when Kelly Geer became my wife.

And the napkin is still around, tucked away in our safe-deposit box.

At the time Kelly wasn't exactly overwhelmed by the gift from her mother. Her response when she received the autograph was "Who's Cal Ripken?" She didn't follow baseball at all and had never been to a game.

But a couple of weeks later, at a promotional appearance, I got a tap on my shoulder. I turned around and this beautiful girl thanked me for being nice to her mother. Before she had the chance to introduce herself, I said, "You must be Kelly."

She was tall, about six feet. Kelly jokes that I was only attracted to her because I wanted sons who would grow up to be basketball players. That's not entirely true; she's also as pretty as her mother.

But I must admit I was impressed when I was over at her apartment and saw her trophy for second place in the statewide "Dribble and Shoot" contest. I'd entered that competition one year, and didn't even make it past the second round. Kelly made it all the way to the finals, which were held at halftime at a Baltimore Bullets (now called the Wizards) game.

There was a snowstorm on the night of our first date, so Kelly and I had dinner at my place with my brother Billy, who was staying with me at the time. We had salsa and chips (all I had on hand) and played cards and darts. It wasn't the most romantic evening in the world, but Kelly and I hit it off. Within a year we were talking about getting engaged.

When it finally came time to propose, I knew it was going to be hard for me to say those four words—"Will you marry me?" So I worked out a plan.

All by myself, with no help from my much more mechanically inclined father or brothers, I rigged up a huge sign using old-fashioned Christmas tree lights. I set it up in the backyard.

It was New Year's Eve. I invited Kelly over for a home-cooked dinner of filet mignon, lobster tails, and champagne. After we were finished eating, I took Kelly up to the balcony on the second floor and asked her what she saw in the yard.

"Nothing," she replied.

"Look again," I suggested, and I flipped a switch. The Christmas lights lit up and spelled out WILL YOU MARRY ME? As she looked at the lights, I took a diamond engagement ring out of my pocket.

My plan worked perfectly, and Kelly's answer was yes. We were married on November 13, 1987.

• A Scare •

About one year after we started dating, Kelly began having headaches, then fainting spells and nausea. She went to several doctors, and each one came up with a different explanation. It was very frustrating.

Kelly was tested for brain tumors, heart problems, cancer, Lyme disease, Hodgkin's disease, and lupus. One doctor diagnosed chronic fatigue syndrome. Another said it was a vertebrae injury.

ABOVE The family home
in Aberdeen

ABOVE Senior in his
early days

RIGHT Born with a bat and
ball in my hands?

ABOVE Family day for the Tri-Cities Atoms. Senior, who managed this minor league team, is kneeling, with (l. to r.) me, Fred, Billy, and Elly.

ABOVE Spring training in Daytona Beach, Florida

LEFT Smiling away at age 7

RIGHT At the park with Mom. From left, Cal, Jr., Elly, and Fred.

BELOW The Aberdeen Indians (1970). I'm second from right, middle row.

LEFT In seventh grade. Still had my hair and a comb in my pocket.

LEFT My freshman year of high school. Guess my growth spurt hadn't kicked in yet.

BELOW At Memorial Stadium with Senior before I was drafted. I'm 16 here.

BELOW Looking good for the prom (1978)

ABOVE My high school team my junior year. I'm third from right, middle row.

LEFT With the Bluefield Orioles in 1978

ABOVE Receiving the MVP for the
second year in a row in the
Caribbean League.
Check out that trophy.

ABOVE In 1981, with the
Rochester Red Wings

RIGHT That's my rival at shortstop,
Bobby Bonner, at a signing with
me in 1981 for the Red Wings.

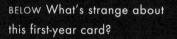

LEFT The family in 1982 after I broke into the big leagues. That's, from the left, Billy, Fred, me, Elly, Senior, and Mom (sitting).

BELOW What's strange about this first-year card?

Cal Ripken, Jr.
ORIOLES • THIRD BASE

ABOVE Earl Weaver steps between Senior and an ump (1979).

RIGHT Our first year together in spring training

LEFT A father-son moment

BELOW 1987

Kelly had to get cortisone shots and hours of neck traction.

Nothing worked. Kelly lost twenty-five pounds. She got light-headed and almost blacked out a few times while driving. She had to quit her job with Piedmont Airlines.

At least a dozen doctors offered opinions. They prescribed twenty-five different medications. Kelly was getting desperate. One doctor decided that Kelly's problem was that she was stressed out from dating a celebrity. He referred her to a psychiatrist. That made her really mad.

"So you're saying Cal is making me sick?" she fumed. "You know what stress is? Stress is not knowing what's wrong. Something is wrong with my body."

But Kelly made an appointment with the psychiatrist anyway, and it was good that she did. Because the psychiatrist asked her if she had ever been tested for Graves' disease, which is a thyroid disorder. She hadn't, which was pretty incredible considering that her mother had Graves'.

Kelly took the tests, and sure enough she was diagnosed with Graves' disease. You can imagine the jumble of emotions for Kelly, her family, and me: relief and frustration.

I'm a "Why?" person, and this is one "Why?" I've never figured out. Graves' disease can be difficult to diagnose, but nobody had ordered a complete thyroid blood test for Kelly.

With a radioactive treatment and daily medica-

LEFT Billy took the number 7 after Senior departed.

BELOW 1982

BELOW Senior at an exhibition game in Nicaragua organized by Dennis Martinez

tion, Graves' disease is controllable. There's no cure, but people who have the disease lead a normal life. Kelly is now a spokeswoman for the American Autoimmune Related Diseases Association.

• Incredible Moments •

I've had many incredible moments in my life, but there have been a few special ones that fans never read about in the papers or saw on TV. The first was when Kelly and I got married.

The second was when my daughter Rachel was born on November 22, 1989. That was the happiest Thanksgiving holiday of my life.

We didn't know if we were having a boy or a girl. We didn't want to know and we didn't care. All we wanted was to hear that first cry. Crying is breathing, a sign of good health. When I saw tiny Rachel and she let out her first big cry, it was amazing.

The third incredible sensation took place on the morning of July 26, 1993, when our second child was born. Again, Kelly and I didn't want to know if we would be having a boy or a girl. So it was a surprise when this big boy arrived. We named him Ryan.

One of the hardest parts about having children is having to leave them. Right after Ryan was born, I had to catch a flight to Toronto for a series against the Blue Jays. Passing out chocolate cigars to my teammates in the clubhouse at the Skydome was a joyful occasion, but it was a little sad too.

8 · The Oriole Way

In the spring of 1988 I was really looking forward to the season ahead. Kelly and I had just been married. Billy would be the Orioles' starting second baseman. Dad would be managing the team again.

Or so I thought.

I was listening to the radio as I was driving to Memorial Stadium on Tuesday, April 12, when the DJ announced that my dad had been fired.

Impossible! My first thought was that the DJ was fooling around. I mean, we had only lost *six* games.

All managers get fired eventually. But after *six games?!* It was the earliest manager firing in baseball history. My *father*.

When I arrived at the clubhouse, Dad had already

left. Billy showed up. Our new manager, Frank Robinson, took Billy and me aside. Frank let us know that he hadn't lobbied for Dad's job. He didn't really even want it, he said. He had the greatest respect for our dad.

I felt deeply for my father. He had been a loyal Oriole man for more than three decades. I couldn't imagine how painful being fired must have been for him. But the harshest thing he said publicly was "I wasn't happy about the thing."

After Dad was gone, we kept losing. Ten games in a row. Fifteen in a row. *Twenty!* The team was confused and disappointed. I was angry. Billy quietly gave up his number 3 uniform and switched to Dad's old number 7.

I had no complaints about Frank Robinson. He was a great player and a fine manager. When I was slumping and the media started saying I should rest a game or two, Frank was totally supportive.

"The easiest part of my job is knowing who I'm going to pencil in for shortstop every day," he kept saying. "I wish I had eight other players like him."

But my disappointment with the Orioles was deep. I kept the emotions inside while trying to sort everything out. When reporters came around asking questions, I kept my mouth shut. All I said was "As a player, I have no opinion. As a son, I'll keep my opinions to myself."

Finally, after twenty-one straight losses, we beat the White Sox in Chicago. When we returned home to Baltimore, more than fifty thousand fans showed up at our next game. That's what I call support.

• A Big Decision •

The Baltimore Orioles have always been considered to be one of the most respected organizations in baseball. There were other great teams, of course, but the Orioles were certainly one of the best. They'd had just one losing year in the twenty-three seasons between 1963 and 1985.

This success came from what we always called "The Oriole Way."

In a nutshell, The Oriole Way is the knowledge, learned over a long period of time, of the best way to teach and play baseball.

The essentials of baseball haven't changed in a hundred years. By now, people who know the game know what works and what doesn't. The Oriole Way is about these fundamentals.

I'll give you an example. Say you've got a runner picked off second base and he makes a dash for third. A lot of other teams instruct their third baseman to jump into the baseline to cut down the distance between himself and the shortstop. The Orioles don't do it that way.

The Oriole Way is to have the third baseman go directly to the third-base bag. The shortstop chases the runner toward third until the runner is moving *too fast* to change direction quickly. Then we nail the runner with one throw to third.

By handling the situation that way, we avoid long back and forth rundowns. Those may be entertaining to watch, but the more a team throws the ball around, the higher the chance that somebody will throw the ball away.

The Orioles teach similar fundamentals for handling cutoff throws, relays, positioning of fielders, and dozens of other situations that come up every day. The system is taught the same way at every level from Rookie League to the majors.

It's not flashy, but it works. It wins games. And the coaches don't have to dream up new plays every spring with the new batch of players.

The Oriole Way also applies to what goes on *off* the field. It means finding, drafting, and developing young talent and keeping it flowing up through the ranks. My dad used to say that if a player could make it all the way through the Oriole system, he would play in the majors. He might not end up with the Orioles, but he would make it with some big league team.

In my early years with the team The Oriole Way was a simple and logical philosophy that worked. It was like a well-tuned engine.

But in 1988, the engine was sputtering. Like my father, I took pride in the Baltimore organization, but the Orioles were changing. That concerned me.

My dad had been fired. Eddie Murray had asked to be traded, and there were rumors that the team was shopping me around. The owner, Edward Bennett Williams, was dying of cancer. Nobody knew what the new owners would have in mind for the future.

The contract I had signed several years earlier was up. I could sign a new contract with the Orioles, or I could make a fresh start with another team. It was one of the toughest decisions I've ever had to make.

Reasons to leave: I was angry about my dad's firing. I was concerned about the decline in the organization I once cherished. I was tired of losing. I wasn't sure I wanted to go through the process of rebuilding.

Reasons to stay: I grew up in the area as an Orioles fan and loved Baltimore. I had made my home in Baltimore and planned to raise my family there. They had traded for Brady Anderson and some other players who could make us contenders in a few years. I could continue to play alongside my brother, and I was young enough to withstand the rebuilding process.

I thought about all these pros and cons, and then thought about them some more. My anger over Dad's firing gradually subsided. The Orioles even hired Dad back as a scout, and Frank Robinson asked him to coach third base the following year.

When he was asked to explain his decision to come back, Dad said simply, "I guess you know I'm an Oriole."

After much soul-searching, I decided to stick with the Orioles.

9 · Rebuilding

Opening Day, 1989. Memorial Stadium in Baltimore. It's the sixth inning. There's one out, two runners on base, and we're trailing 3-1.

I'm facing one of the best pitchers in baseball—Roger Clemens of the defending American League East champions, the Boston Red Sox. Nicknamed "The Rocket," Clemens had fanned me in the second inning on hundred-mile-per-hour fastballs, the kind that sometimes give a hitter nightmares.

The count is two balls and two strikes. I foul off a couple of pitches before Roger tries a high fastball that tails just a bit over the plate. I take a rip at it and connect.

As I watch the ball soar over the wall, the fans go wild and my heart is pounding. *Really* pounding. What a way to start the season!

Just as the team that wins the World Series is expected to do well the next season, the team with the worst record in baseball is expected to do poorly again.

Well, from Opening Day on, we surprised everyone in 1989. Despite the fact that Eddie Murray was gone and we had thirteen rookies on the team, we won ball games. And we just kept winning.

In July we led the American League East by seven games. For 116 days we held on to first place. We slipped after that, but bounced back and went to Toronto the last weekend of the season trailing the Blue Jays by just one game. If we could sweep the three game series, we'd win the division.

It didn't happen. We were one pitch away from winning the first game when the Blue Jays came back and won it in the eleventh inning.

The fairy-tale year—and the decade of the 1980s—was over. We didn't win the pennant, but the Orioles had shown signs of life.

• Boooooooooooo! •

Because I was born in 1960, the start of every new decade is also the start of a new decade for *me*. In 1990 I turned thirty, which is a significant turning point for anybody, especially an athlete.

At the start of the season I went into a deep slump. My average was in the low .200s—not good, even for a shortstop. The fans booed me after a

63

strikeout on June 11, the day I tied Everett Scott for second place on the consecutive games list (1,307).

All players get booed sometimes. At the beginning of my career it really bothered me. Eventually, I came to the realization that fan reaction isn't personal. A boo is a reaction of displeasure. It doesn't mean the fan dislikes *me*. He dislikes what I *did*.

Similarly, when I hit a homer, the fan is not necessarily cheering *me*. He's cheering my home run. I do the same thing when I'm watching sports on TV.

It's easy for an athlete to forget there's a difference between him and his performance on the field. When I get booed, I keep reminding myself that it isn't personal and not to worry about it.

Still, a slump wears you down. I tried not to look at the scoreboard when I was at the plate. I knew what my batting average was, but I couldn't bear to see it up in lights. There it was, even if I didn't look, almost like a nightmare: .209 . . . .209 . . . .209.

Finally, my manager Frank Robinson called me into his office one day. He told me that when *he* turned thirty in 1965, he had a bad slump too. People started describing him as an "old thirty."

But he snapped out of his slump. The next year Frank won the Triple Crown (most homers, RBIs, and highest average in the league). He was sure I would snap out of my slump too.

Frank reminded me that slumps are part of the

game. A .300 hitter doesn't hit .300 all the time. He might hit .300 for a week. The next week he might hit .400. The week after that he might go into a slump and hit .200. It all averages out. That's why it's a batting *average*.

The same thing happens over the course of a career. One season you hit .330. The next season you hit .270. Together, they average out to .300.

Just as Reggie Jackson's encouragement had helped me get out of my rookie slump, talking with Frank Robinson helped me in 1990. He also pumped up my ego by telling me I was the only guy he'd ever seen who could hit a home run off a batting tee. (I've never seen anyone else do it either.)

We tinkered with my batting stance too, and eventually I broke out of the slump. For the rest of the season I hit about .300.

The Orioles slumped too in 1990, finishing eleven and a half games out of first place. Not great, but we had been through a lot worse.

• Total Dedication •

After the 1990 season I noticed some personal statistics I didn't like. For my first six seasons I'd averaged about twenty-six homers. For the next three seasons I dropped to twenty-one. My RBIs dropped from ninety-five to eighty-six in the same period. My batting average slipped too.

I thought about those numbers and felt I had to do something. If my physical skills had begun to deteriorate with age, there wasn't much I could do about it. But I wasn't ready to accept that.

So in the off-season I decided to rededicate myself to conditioning my body. I've always taken care of myself and worked out in the off-season, but now because of an uncertainty about aging, there was a more concentrated effort. A more structured workout program. *Total* dedication.

My entire career—my entire *life*, really—I had dreamed of building my own gym. As a kid I used to run in the house after shooting baskets in the winter cold and my hands would be frozen. Mom would say that when I grew up, I could buy a farm and convert the barn into a gym with a basketball court.

In 1990, I built a gym adjacent to my house. Besides the basketball court, I put in a batting cage, a weight room, and even a locker room. Kelly topped the whole thing off with a great Christmas present for me—an electronic scoreboard. The gym cost quite a bit of money, but I figured that if it extended my career just one year, it would pay for itself many times over.

On just about every day of the off-season I organized a game at my gym. Guys on the Orioles would come over to play, as well as other baseball players, ex-college basketball players, and semi-pros. All kinds of athletes would show up. There were traffic jams in the driveway.

Often, we'd turn the basketball court into a street-hockey rink. A group of us had discovered the joy of that sport while messing around in the Oriole clubhouse. We'd turn the tables on their sides to make "boards" and run around in our sneakers with bats and balls. We'd tear the place up and then put everything back when we were done.

It got pretty physical. I dislocated my finger once after getting smashed into a wall. But street hockey is terrific exercise.

When I wasn't playing in one game or another, I'd hit balls off a tee or thrown by a pitching machine. I'd throw baseballs against the wall, or lift weights.

A baseball player should keep in mind that he has specific baseball needs, and should always mix his skill work with his weight training. Remember that you are a baseball player and not a professional weight lifter. Lifting should *enhance* your baseball skills, so take it easy, listen to your body, and use common sense. My goal is to be in the best shape when I arrive at spring training.

• The Contest •

When I arrived for spring training in 1991, I was in the best shape of my life. I had a great spring, and got off to a good start. By the All-Star break I was leading the league with a .348 average.

I'm not a slugger, but I was hitting so well that I had eighteen homers at that point. That qualified me for the home run hitting contest they hold the day before the All-Star game. I was excited, but also a little concerned. I didn't want to mess up my swing by trying to hit home runs.

I decided to just swing naturally. If I didn't hit any out of the park, that would be fine. In batting practice, I couldn't hit one out, so I wasn't expecting much.

Here's the way home run hitting contests usually work: A bunch of hitters face batting practice pitching. If you swing at a pitch, anything except a homer is an "out." Each hitter is allowed ten outs. The guy with the most homers is the winner.

As I stepped into the batter's box, the big crowd at the Toronto Skydome was buzzing and cheering. I took a few pitches, then hit a screaming line drive into the camera stand in dead center field. That got my attention.

I turned to our dugout and held up a finger to signal, THAT'S ONE. Then came two, then three, then four. At one point I hit seven in a row!

I was in this incredible groove, swinging effortlessly. The balls were going as far as I'd ever hit them. The other All-Stars were on the top step of the dugout, yelling and screaming.

The final result: twelve homers on twenty-two swings. I was the first shortstop ever to win the home run hitting contest. The guys kidded me about the baseballs being juiced up. But I was just in one sweet groove that day.

The All-Star Game was just as sweet. I came up in the third inning and slammed a pitch from

Dennis Martinez over the center field fence for
three-run homer. The American League won, 4-

• Good Luck •

I tried three new things that year, which may
may not have contributed to my success. First,
got a laptop computer and used it to plot how I h
against various pitchers. It was fun, and helpe
me learn about computers too.

Second, I was forced to retire my favorite glov
For two years I had been using a Rawlings Pr
6HF. It had a huge pocket, which was great t
snare spinning bouncers and easy to get the ba
out of to turn double plays.

One day the webbing ripped halfway ou
Rawlings did an emergency leather transplant i
a desperate attempt to save the glove. The patien
survived, but it was never the same again. I had t
put it to sleep.

Third, I got some new bats. Throughout m
career, I never changed the weight or length o
my bats very much. But every year I would change
the *finish*. Some years I'd order light-brown bats
Other years I'd hit with bare wood. That year, jus
for the heck of it, I ordered black bats.

Some hitters believe a black bat is harder for the
fielders to track, because they can't see the ball
coming off it as well. Others say it doesn't make
any difference.

I can't say for sure whether my black bats brought

me good luck or not, but they certainly didn't hurt. I finished the season with career highs in average (.323), home runs (thirty-four), and RBIs (114) while striking out only forty-six times. It was only the tenth time in history that a player hit thirty home runs with fewer than fifty strikeouts.

To top it all off, I earned my first Gold Glove and second Most Valuable Player Award. Frank Robinson was right. I wasn't an "old thirty."

As for the Orioles, we didn't come close in 1991. The team was still in the rebuilding phase, and it had yet to produce results.

• The End of an Era •

The only other sad thing about 1991 was that it was the last season for Baltimore's Memorial Stadium. The pile of bricks on Thirty-third Street certainly wasn't the prettiest park in the league, but everyone loved it.

We all knew something special was scheduled to take place after the last out in the last game at Memorial (made by me, by the way). We just didn't know *what*.

A strange silence hung in the air after the game was over. The fans stayed in their seats.

Suddenly, a white stretch limousine drove onto the field. The grounds crew got out—wearing tuxedos. They dug up home plate and drove away with it. Then there was more anxious silence.

The theme music from the baseball movie *Field*

of Dreams filled the stadium. Then James Earl Jones's famous "Build it and they will come" speech from the movie was heard.

As the music continued, Brooks Robinson—my boyhood hero—trotted out of the dugout with his glove and took his old position at third base. There was no introduction. Everybody knew who he was.

Then Frank Robinson jogged out to right field, *his* old position. Boog Powell came out next, then Jim Palmer . . . Don Baylor . . . Rick Dempsey. Dozens of former Orioles streamed out of the dugout one at a time to take their old positions on the field.

I waited my turn in the clubhouse, covered with goose bumps. I was the next-to-last Oriole to leave the dugout. Earl Weaver, who had guided all these players through so many great seasons, got the honor of being last.

All 118 of us formed a huge circle around the infield to honor the fans. Rick Dempsey led one final O-R-I-O-L-E-S cheer and we all threw baseballs into the stands.

On the Diamondvision screen we watched the grounds crew deliver home plate to its new home at Camden Yards across town. Announcer Rex Barney, who was propped up in a hospital bed, gave his signature line, "THANK Youuuu." Finally, everyone sang "Auld Lang Syne."

It was a memory to last a lifetime.

10 · A New Spirit

I always loved old Memorial Stadium. But when Oriole Park at Camden Yards opened in the spring of 1992, I loved it too. The place was a great mix of modern baseball (skyboxes, big screen, better sight lines) with an old-time feeling of coziness (the B&O warehouse, Bromo-Seltzer clock tower, irregularly shaped outfield).

We had a new ballpark, a new manager in Johnny Oates, some new guys who could play, and a new spirit as a team. There was real confidence at spring training. You could feel it.

Our pitching staff banded together and started calling themselves The Posse. "Don't mess with The Posse," they would say. On one occasion they got together and tied me to the training table. They also "de-pantsed" Brady Anderson right on the field during a practice session.

In the first game at Camden Yards my brother dropped down a perfect suicide squeeze bunt and we shut out Cleveland 2-0. We went on to win ten of our first eleven games at home.

We couldn't keep that pace all season, of course. But we played well. In late August we were a half game behind Toronto. Then the Blue Jays poured it on while we were slumping, and suddenly it was all over. We finished seven games back. But we won twenty-two games more than we did the year before, and everyone on the team considered it a great season.

• That's Baseball •

I wish I could say the same for my own performance. After a great 1991 I was looking forward to another good season. Instead, I struggled all year.

The Orioles and I were negotiating my contract for a good part of the year, and I made the mistake of letting the business side of the game affect the baseball side. I wasn't focused, and it showed in my statistics. Though I won my second Gold Glove, my average plummeted to .251, homers dropped to a career low fourteen, and I only drove in seventy-two runs.

To make things worse, after the season was over, the Orioles let go of my father *and* my brother. I realistically knew the three of us couldn't be on the same team forever. Still, it hurts when guys go, especially when they're members of your own family.

For Dad, it was the second time the Orioles had fired him. I didn't know exactly why, and I still don't. He probably could have gotten a coaching job in another organization, but Dad decided it was time to retire from the game he loved so much.

For Billy, getting released was probably even harder. At least Dad had some finality. Billy (who was released on his twenty-eighth birthday) only had six years of experience. After a few anxious months when the phone wasn't ringing, Billy was receiving interest from two teams. He eventually signed with the Texas Rangers.

As luck would have it, the Orioles hosted the Rangers on Opening Day of 1993. It was kind of strange to watch Billy trot out of the *visitors* dugout wearing a *different* uniform during the opening ceremonies.

We had grown up together, teased and tussled together, and started side by side in 634 major league games. And now we were opponents. But that's baseball.

Especially in recent years, baseball organizations constantly change from one year to the next. Players are shuffled on and off the roster. Trades are made. Players become free agents. Guys retire or get hurt. New guys are always coming up from the minors.

Coaches and managers are unceremoniously dumped when teams do poorly. Sometimes they get dumped even when the team does *well*.

The reasoning behind these decisions is not always clear. An organization might get rid of all its best people simply because it doesn't want to pay their big salaries.

Despite all this turmoil, each year one team combines enough skill with enough luck to reach the World Series. The Orioles hadn't been to the Series since we'd won it in my second season. I wanted to get back there.

• Playing the Field •

I mentioned that in 1992, my batting average dropped to .251. It's bounced around a lot during my career—in fact, it once went from .250 to .323 in consecutive seasons. But I like to think my play in the field has been rock solid year after year.

Hitting usually gets most of the attention. But in professional baseball, pitching and defense win games. This has been true in every winning season I've played.

I'm not flashy with the glove. You don't see me making many "circus" catches when they show game highlights. My style is considered normal, efficient, maybe even boring. But I take as much pride in my defense as anything I've accomplished with the bat.

Over the years I have led the American League

in various defensive categories and won the Gold Glove award twice. In 1990 I set four major league records for shortstops: consecutive errorless games (95), consecutive errorless chances (431), fewest errors in a season (3), and highest fielding percentage (.996).

Shortstop and third base, the two positions I have played, look similar at first glance. But they're actually quite different.

Because the ball gets to third ("the hot corner") more quickly, a third baseman has more time to make a play on a sharp grounder. So you can dive to stop the ball, then get to your feet and make the throw to first to catch even the fastest runner. You develop a hockey goalie-type mentality.

Shortstops rarely have time for that. By the time they dive, pop up, and throw, the runner has probably crossed first base. If that happens, there was really no point in diving for the ball in the first place (assuming the bases were empty).

The biggest compliment I've received about my fielding is that I make the hard plays look easy. I study the pitchers. I study the hitters. So I'm usually in the right position and don't *have* to make a diving grab. If I read the ball off the bat well and do my job, the play appears to be routine.

I play this way because I *have* to. I'm not as quick on my feet as some other guys. So I use my head. Over the years I've learned techniques to get my body in position to throw more quickly.

Sometimes you look flashy, no matter what. When there's a bunt down the foul line, the third baseman sometimes has no choice but to pick it up bare-handed and whip a sidearm, falling-down throw to first. Fortunately a shortstop may only need to make a play like that a few times each season.

Bare-handing the ball is a risk. I've seen short-stops bare-hand two-hoppers with topspin on arti-ficial turf. It's easy to miss the ball when you do that, and it's easy to break a finger too. That's why we wear gloves. I follow this maxim: If the ball's moving, catch it with your glove.

The shortstop is usually more involved in the game than the third baseman. At third you can't see the catcher's signs. You're not a part of as many steals, hit-and-runs, coverages, or relays. If the ball isn't hit to you, often the play is finished as far as you're concerned. Sometimes there's a feeling of standing and watching, almost like a spectator. The shortstop, on the other hand, is right in the thick of things.

Say there's a runner on first. There are so many things the shortstop has to think about:

Who will cover second base on a steal attempt? Is the hitter in a slump, and more likely to take an outside pitch? Does he pull the first pitch? Is he a good hit-and-run batter? Is this a hit-and-run count? If the catcher sets up outside, is the pitch-er likely to hit the target? Is his control good enough? Does he change speed on his fastball on certain counts? What does the opposing manager usually do in this situation?

Every pitch is a new world. You have to be thinking all the time. For me, this is the real fun and challenge of baseball.

11 · *The Streak*

On May 31, 1925, a twenty-one-year-old ballplayer stepped out of the New York Yankee dugout and
jogged out to first base. His name was Lou Gehrig.
We never met, of course, but I'm proud that his
name and my name are linked together forever.

Gehrig's teammate, the great Babe Ruth, got
most of the headlines. But Lou Gehrig was out
there every day, putting up his own incredible
numbers. He had a .340 lifetime batting average.
He hit 493 homers, including four in one game.
One season he drove in 184 runs.

His most famous number was 2,130—the number
of games he played in a row. Over thirteen seasons
"The Iron Horse" played every game, at one point
or another leading the American League in runs,
hits, doubles, triples, homers, RBIs, batting average, and slugging percentage.

But something happened to Lou Gehrig in 1938. His average dipped below .300 for the first time in thirteen years. He hit fewer than thirty homers for the first time in a decade. He moved more slowly in the field and on the base paths. It was more than aging. Something was wrong.

The next spring Gehrig could hardly play. After a few games he told his manager that he was taking himself out of the lineup. His streak ended on May 2, 1939.

Lou Gehrig didn't take a day off to rest. He was never able to play again.

Tests were done and it was discovered that Gehrig had a rare form of paralysis called amyotrophic lateral sclerosis. Later, it came to be known as "Lou Gehrig's disease." There was no cure for it. There still isn't.

Lou Gehrig died two years later, a couple of weeks before his thirty-eighth birthday. It was a tragedy.

• The Streak and Me •

I never made it my goal to break Lou Gehrig's consecutive games record. All I ever wanted to do was play every day, as best as I could. But when I reached 1,000 consecutive games (on July 25, 1988), people started talking about *my* streak in relation to Gehrig's streak.

At the end of the 1990 season I was at 1,411 games. The more I played, the more people talked about the streak. It zapped my spirit a little. In times past, I'd always laughed when Kirby Puckett pulled up at second base after yet another double and called out to me, "Cheer up, Cal, just four more years and you can have a rest!" By 1993, maybe I wasn't laughing very hard.

It was funny, but not true. I could take a rest anytime I wanted to. But I didn't *want* to. I still wanted to play every day.

Many people supported me and what was happening. But as the streak got longer, I began to catch a lot of criticism too. It wasn't the same old Cal-should-take-a-day-off criticism. Articles started coming out and saying I was *obsessed* with Lou Gehrig's record. I was being selfish by playing every day.

A former player was quoted as saying, "He's hurting the team and showing that personal goals are more important. He wants to break Lou Gehrig's record even if it costs Baltimore the pennant."

It wasn't true, of course. But it still bothered me.

As it happened, I was in a deep batting slump at the start of the 1993 season, which only made the criticism worse. I was getting seriously worn down.

I asked myself, *Am I still doing the right thing by playing every day? Maybe I should take a day off.* I didn't think I *needed* a day off, but maybe all the talk of the streak would stop if I just ended it.

On the other hand, I didn't want to do something just because *other* people said I should. Sitting down for a game or two wouldn't make a difference. It wouldn't improve my hitting. It might even make the slump *worse*. To me, giving in to critics would be running away from the problem instead of facing it.

One day during batting practice, I walked over to our pitcher Rick Sutcliffe, whom I really respect and admire. I asked Rick if he thought I was doing the right thing. I admitted that I was considering taking a day off.

Rick looked at me as if it was the dumbest thing he had ever heard. He told me that the team *needed* me in the lineup, and they needed me in the middle of the field every day.

"I'm pitching tomorrow night," Rick said, "and your name is going to be in the paper one way or another. You're either going to be in the lineup, or in the obituaries."

I kept playing.

• The Day the Streak Almost Ended •

On June 6, 1993, we were playing Seattle at home. A couple of our hitters got knocked down by pitches. When our pitcher Mike Mussina hit one of the Seattle guys, both benches emptied. Punches were thrown. It turned into a baseball brawl.

I was running toward the mound to help protect Mike when my foot slipped. I heard a pop in my right knee. The next thing I knew, a few thousand pounds of players were on top of me. When I got up, the knee felt a little tender, but I stayed in the game.

When I woke up the next morning and put my right foot on the floor, I winced. I couldn't put any weight on it. My first reaction was, *There's no way I can play tonight.*

"Couldn't you just play one inning?" Kelly asked.

Lou Gehrig, I had been informed, did that a number of times. In game number 1,427 he led off with a single and a pinch runner replaced him. He was through for the day. Gehrig played just one inning in three other games. In two games he played just two innings. Many times he left a game before it was over.

But so what? I was never competing with Lou Gehrig anyway. I just wanted to play ball every day. And the way my knee felt, I wasn't sure I could walk to my kitchen, much less play an inning.

I limped to the phone and called the Oriole trainer, Richie Bancells. "I think I have a problem," I told him.

Richie advised me to put ice on the knee and meet him at the ballpark early. He called a doctor. I called my parents and they came over right away.

The doctor told me I had a sprained ligament, which is a band of tissue that connects two bones. The injury would limit my lateral movement, which is not good. A shortstop needs to move from side to side.

The game was scheduled to start in five hours. Richie went to work. He soaked the knee in a cold whirlpool. He stimulated the muscle. He hit it with ultrasound. Word spread around the clubhouse, and my teammates peeked into the trainer's room to see how I was doing.

After three hours Richie had done all he could do for me. I put on my uniform and went out on the field to test the knee. It didn't feel that bad. I jogged a little, did a couple of sprints, and tried some quick starts and stops. I took a few swings in the batting cage and fielded some ground balls. The knee felt pretty good. Not a hundred percent, but pretty good.

I was aware of the risks. If I went out on the field and completely tore the ligament, a mild injury would become a major one that would keep me off the field for a long time.

What I didn't realize at the time was how much pressure everyone was feeling that day. My manager, Johnny Oates, didn't want to become known as the guy who'd ended Cal Ripken's streak. Neither did the trainer or the doctor. In the end it was my decision.

Ten minutes before game time I stuck my head in Johnny Oates's office. "It's a go," I said.

I was tested early in the game—the first batter hit a hopper in the hole with topspin on it. I dashed over and gloved it, planted my right foot, and threw him out at first. I was going to be okay.

I ended up running the bases three times and playing the whole game. I knew I'd made the right decision. The ligament healed and I was able to keep playing.

At the end of the 1993 season I had played in 1,897 consecutive games.

Some people say that to play in so many games, I must have a bionic body. Not at all.

Besides that knee injury, I've had lots of painful twists and bruises and strains during my career. Foul balls have ricocheted off my ankles. I've sprained them so many times that they click as I walk.

Once my nose got broken while I was getting my picture taken at the All-Star game! White Sox reliever Roberto Hernandez fell off the bleachers and accidentally whacked me in the face as he was going down.

None of those injuries knocked me out of the lineup. I heal quickly. I stay in good shape because I do what the doctors and trainers tell me to do. And to a certain extent, I've been lucky. For all those reasons I've been fortunate to avoid a major injury in my career.

• The Streak and the Strike •

On August 1, 1994, I had played my 2,000th consecutive game. All during that season, the players and owners were going through one of our periodic labor disputes.

I won't bore you with all the details. But I was in my car one day when I heard on the radio that the owners had decided to cancel the end of the regular season and the World Series.

85

The World Series!? Baseball hadn't missed a World Series in ninety years! The Orioles were in second place at the time, with a chance to win our division. I was stunned and angry and sad.

The owners were threatening to start the 1995 season with "replacement players" if we couldn't resolve our differences by Opening Day. They would hire college players, minor leaguers, and retired players to take the place of the major leaguers.

I made it clear that games with replacement players would not be major league baseball, and I wouldn't play in those games. Standing with my fellow players was more important than continuing the streak.

The owner of the Orioles, Peter Angelos, announced that he would *not* field a team of replacement players no matter what. He said he would forfeit every Oriole game if he had to. Angelos was the only owner to say that. I saw it as a strong show of support for me and the team, and I appreciated it.

As it turned out, the dispute was settled. No replacement players were used, and I was able to continue playing every day.

• Good News •

The strike in 1994 was terrible for baseball. A great season was ruined, and the game was going to have to do some serious rebuilding to earn back the faith of the fans. Baseball needed some good

LEFT With Kirby Puckett at Memorial Stadium around 1990

ABOVE With Ryan in the pool

ABOVE Teaching Rachel the finer aspects of the game at Camden Yards

RIGHT Family reunion at Camden Yards

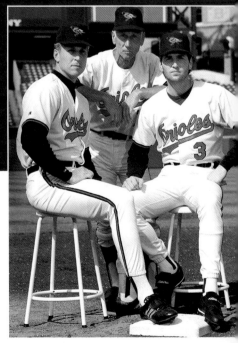

ABOVE With Eddie Murray

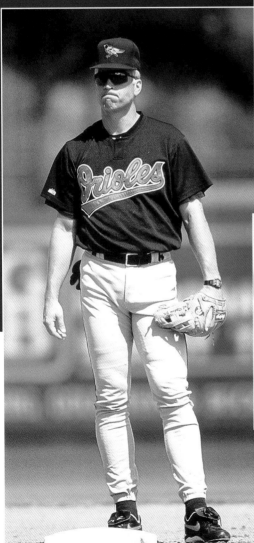

STREAK NIGHT 2131

LEFT AND BELOW
My home run in the
Streak Game

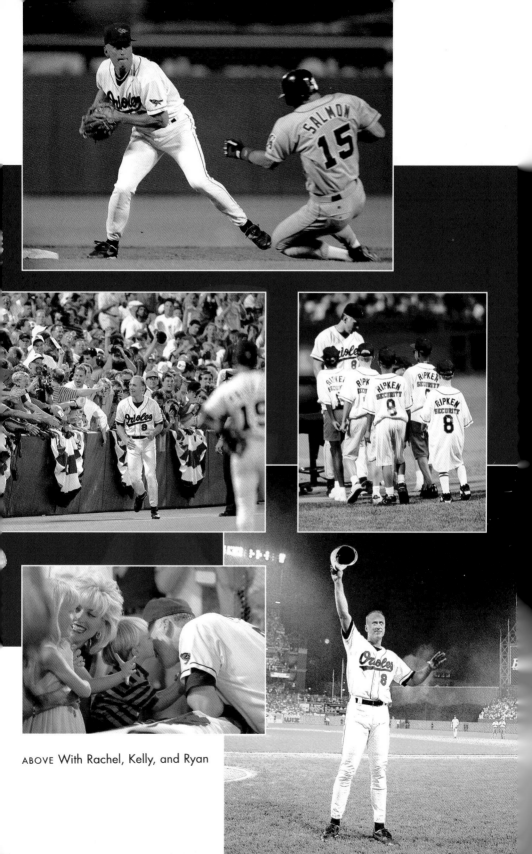

ABOVE With Rachel, Kelly, and Ryan

news. To a lot of people, I guess, my streak provided that.

Around the time I played my 2,000th consecutive game, it became apparent that people openly wanted me to break the record. The streak became a very positive thing. Fans around the country—not just in Baltimore—*wanted* me to go for the record.

Before, Gehrig's record had seemed unreachable to me. Now the number 2,000 made the number 2,131 seem much closer. For the first time, I really understood that it was possible.

12 · Fame

From the first day of spring training in 1995 I realized my life would never be the same again. When I walked on the field in Sarasota, Florida, photographers and reporters were everywhere. It was chaos. Bedlam.

I was still 121 games short of Lou Gehrig's mark, but the media was all over me as if I was going to break the record that day.

From that moment on the phone rang off the hook. Mail poured in. Cars drove past Mom and Dad's house. People got out and asked them for autographs. Reporters wanted to interview my wife and brothers and sister. My old roommate Floyd Rayford said he did seventy-five interviews about me over the summer.

Every aspect of the streak was covered. There

were articles about Ernie Tyler, the Camden Yards umpire attendant. (On the night I broke the record, Ernie was up to 2,810 consecutive games.) *USA Today* did a feature on Herbert Christiansen, who had worked in a Chicago hardware store every day for fifty-nine years. Now *that's* a streak!

Fame is a funny thing. Once I was a regular guy who could go anywhere he wanted and nobody would notice him. Then one day, it seemed, I couldn't go anywhere without someone noticing me.

In the beginning of my career I did a lot of personal appearances everywhere—shopping centers, lumberyards, you name it. I felt this work was part of the responsibility of being a major league ballplayer.

But as my career progressed, I became overwhelmed with requests for appearances. I couldn't do them all. There simply wasn't enough time. I was forced to learn how to sometimes say, "No, thank you."

But for those of us who are in the public eye, *every* time we go outside, it's an "appearance." Occasionally people will go through extreme measures to track down ballplayers. It's no secret where the team stays when we're on the road.

Once someone checked into our hotel and convinced the front desk they were relatives of mine. Then they checked into the two rooms on either side of my room and left both doors open so that they would know whenever I went anywhere or returned to my room.

Once, in Texas, I left my room at one o'clock in the morning to get some ice from the ice machine in the hall. Suddenly I saw a blurry movement. A guy leaped out from behind the ice machine. He was holding a baseball bat. For a moment I thought he might to club me.

As it turned out, he just wanted me to autograph the bat! Who knows how long he would have waited for me to come out of my room?

Radio stations are always calling players' hotel rooms early in the morning. My brother Billy used to get this all the time. He would be fast asleep and pick up the ringing phone thinking it must be an emergency. Then some really perky guy would shout, "This is your wake-up call!"

"I didn't ask for a wake-up call," Billy would moan. "I don't *want* a wake-up call."

"Well, this is WUFO, and *you're on the air!*"

For all these reasons, beginning in 1993 I started staying in a different hotel than the Orioles in some cities. People don't understand, so I've sometimes been criticized for doing this, but I just needed some peace. Call it a weakness if you will— I do—but staying elsewhere is much more peaceful than staying at the team hotel.

For the ten or more hours I'm at the ballpark, I give everything I've got to baseball. So do the other guys. Beforehand and afterward I need my time to regroup. I'm that kind of person.

A few people have said that my staying at a different hotel affects the team chemistry. I don't see it. When the team is playing at home—which is half the season—we all stay in different homes. Does this affect team chemistry, or is there chemistry only on the road?

• Fame and Family •

Fame can be hardest on a person's loved ones. When I went into professional baseball, I pretty much knew what to expect. But when Kelly married me, all the attention took her by surprise. She was considered *Mrs. Cal Ripken*, not Kelly Ripken. When she met people, they would often talk about me, or about the Orioles, or about baseball.

At one of the first games she went to after we were married, a guy came over and asked Kelly if he could kiss her on the cheek because his friends were watching. At that stage Kelly was sort of a soft touch and agreed. Then, a couple of other guys made the same request. By the fifth inning Kelly had a new rule. *No kissing.*

Raising kids with a husband who's more or less gone for seven months a year isn't easy. Like every other couple, we do our best to hold everything together. Kelly has handled the situation amazingly well. She's strong; she deals with it. We have a wonderful life together.

I figure there's enough baseball in our lives as it

is, so I try to leave the game at the park. I stay in the clubhouse a long time after each game, reflecting on it, maybe getting rid of bad feelings. That way, I don't have to burden the family with it when I get home.

During the off-season, Kelly and I have a "date night" every week. It's usually dinner and a movie. I wait in the car while Kelly gets the tickets and the popcorn. Then she gives me a sign and I hurry into the theater.

Date night is a great escape. On those nights I'm just a husband.

Similarly, when I take my kids to an activity, I want to be there just as their father. If someone asks for an autograph, I say, "I'm just Rachel and Ryan's dad right now. I hope you understand."

I don't do that to protect myself from signing. I do it because it needs to be Rachel and Ryan's activity, not an extension of my life as a ballplayer. Most of the time people understand. Sometimes they don't.

One thing that's difficult is teaching my kids about strangers. Kelly and I want Rachel and Ryan to feel that the world is a good, safe place. But we also want them to be careful regarding strangers.

The thing is, a lot of "strangers" say hi to me. When a fan greets me, Rachel often asks, "Is *he* a stranger?" I have to answer, "Well, yes." It's confusing to her and Ryan. They see everyone as a friend, which would be a wonderful way to look at the world—if this were a perfect world.

• Autographs •

I didn't collect many autographs when I was a kid, and I certainly could have, hanging around the clubhouse with my dad. I've never really understood why it means so much to people to have a name signed on a piece of paper.

But I realize that autographing goes with the territory. It's a part of baseball. I don't fight it. I accept it, and I actually enjoy it.

When I give a kid an autograph and his face lights up, that makes the whole thing go. How many opportunities do most people have to make someone so happy for even a brief moment? This is the beauty of the relationship between fans and players.

There's an organization called Make-A-Wish for kids who have life-threatening diseases. I see that look in the eyes of the Make-A-Wish kids when I meet them before ball games. Their stories are heartbreaking. I try to focus on the here and now, just like they're trying to do. If I can help make things better for them and their families, I will.

Early in my career I would sit in my car in the parking lot after games and sign autographs for an hour or more. That became unmanageable at a certain point, so I shifted my signing to inside the stadium.

I think I've signed just about everything there is to sign: balls, bats, baseball cards, photos, magazines, ticket stubs, caps, business cards, gloves, dollar bills, pennants, Wheaties boxes. When a kid hands me a smashed popcorn box with sneaker prints on it, I know that can have only one purpose: holding a real memory for someone, maybe for a lifetime.

"Please! Please!" I can hear the anxiety behind the voice when people gather around. Maybe they've been waiting for a long time. Maybe they're being crushed by other fans. I do my best to get to as many as I can. I'm happy and willing to give people as much time as possible. But I hope they understand that I do have to leave eventually and I might not be able to get to everyone.

I *don't* like being overly targeted by baseball memorabilia dealers who hire kids to get autographs. But I see it happen. I'll sign something for a kid, and he disappears into a crowd. Then I see another kid come out of the same spot and ask me to sign an identical item. I know there's a dealer over there paying kids a few bucks per autograph so that he can turn around and sell the items at a profit. I don't think it's right.

Most of the time you just can't tell the difference between a true collector and somebody who's only in it for the money. There are lots of forgeries and scams out there. So you have to be careful. If you didn't get it directly from me, make sure it's from an authorized company.

When I'm with my family, I can't sign autographs. At that time I'm just trying my best to be a good daddy and husband.

• Heroes •

I kind of understand hero worship, because I've looked at other athletes that way. I like basketball, and from time to time put a few players up on a pedestal. I know Michael Jordan is a regular guy, but because of his great talent I just don't look at him that way.

People think the life of a "celebrity" is more exciting than their own. But in the end, it's not true. In fact, I'm pretty sure that my life isn't any more exciting than most people's lives. It may be more *complicated*. For someone like me who prefers order, this can be uncomfortable.

I was in a restaurant once and the waitress asked me, "Are you a very famous person?"

"Depends on what you mean," I said.

"Is your name Carl?"

"Cal."

"Oh, right . . . but you're such a *nice* person!"

People must think that if you're "famous," you must be egotistical, impolite, maybe even arrogant. I can't speak for anybody else, but I'm still a regular guy. I changed my kids' diapers when they were little. When stuff breaks down around the house, I try to fix it. Fame hasn't changed me. It's always a pleasure to hear someone call me Calvin: They knew me before I became a professional baseball player.

Being recognized has its drawbacks, and it has its benefits. For me, fame is not nearly as big a deal as a lot of people apparently believe. I wouldn't have any problem if suddenly I wasn't famous anymore.

My brother Fred is a great motorcycle mechanic. A reporter once asked him if he was envious of me. That made me smile, because at times I've been a little jealous and envious of *him*.

Before I met Kelly, Fred was already married and had a child. I felt he had discovered a certain happiness and peace. He had the secret.

• My Surrender •

As I got closer to Lou Gehrig's record of 2,130 consecutive games, the attention paid to me and the streak became unbelievable. Up until 1995 I was a ballplayer. But suddenly, I was being written about like a sort of national institution, like apple pie.

Coming right after the labor dispute that hurt baseball so much, I think my situation became an opportunity for people to express their good feelings about the game. They were angry at the owners and the players because of the strike, but they still loved baseball. The streak seemed to tie modern baseball and "the good old days" together.

For years I had resisted making a big deal of the streak. All the attention people gave it was embarrassing to me.

"For once in your life, enjoy it," Kelly told me as I approached Lou Gehrig's record. "Let them tell you how great you are. Go with the flow."

As I closed in on game 2,130, I came to realize that the streak was a good thing for the game of baseball. I decided to stop wasting my energy fighting all the attention. Instead, I surrendered to the celebration.

13 · *Breaking the Record*

As soon as our game was official on August 29, 1995, an enormous number 2,123 was lowered onto the brick wall of the old warehouse just beyond the right field fence at Camden Yards. The number on the wall made everything very real. Eight games to go. It hit me hard. For the first time I felt real pressure. If all went according to plan, I would tie the record on September 5 and break it on September 6.

The Orioles were on a long home stand against the West Coast teams. Number 2,131 was scheduled to be the final game. The Orioles wanted me to break the record at home. So did I. Of course, if any of our games got rained out or postponed, the record would have been broken on the road.

Game 2,124 . . . 2,125 . . . 2,126 . . .

When each game was declared an official game, a new number was unfurled on the brick wall and the fans went crazy. I was usually on the field when this happened. It was a little embarrassing. I didn't know what to do other than doff my cap.

As the crowd was cheering, moments from my career would flash through my mind. I remembered things I hadn't thought about for years. It became a time of reflection. When the more emotional memories came up, I tried to fight those back. I didn't want to break down in the middle of a crucial game. I did my best to focus on baseball.

Game 2,127 . . . 2,128 . . . 2,129 . . .

As we approached the final games, the press was crawling all over Camden Yards. Cameras followed me on the field. The Orioles handed out 750 press badges during those last games. The team had to set up a locker in a separate room away from the clubhouse so that interviews could take place without disturbing the other players. We put uniforms, gloves, shoes, and other stuff inside to make it look like a real locker.

Ever since game 2,000 I had been treated so wonderfully by everyone that I decided to reciprocate by signing as many autographs as possible after games. The crowd started lining up in the third inning above our dugout on the first-base line.

Some nights, by the end of the game, the line snaked all the way up through the box seats and out through the concession arcade.

Unfortunately, sometimes things got out of hand. After two women got into a fistfight, the Orioles had to call off the post-game signing sessions.

A few days before game 2,130, I started to work on my thank-you speech. I'd given a lot of speeches over the years. But not like this. There would be a full house at Camden Yards and millions of people in the national television audience.

I was a little worried about the echo effect of the public-address system. It takes a moment or two to broadcast your words after you say them. That becomes confusing when you're speaking. I also worried about whether I'd be able to thank my parents and family without my emotions getting the better of me.

It would have been great if the Orioles were in the pennant race when I broke the record. That way, the focus would have been on the ball game, where it belonged. We had a chance in July, but unfortunately we were pretty much out of it by mid-August.

Honestly, I would have traded all the hoopla for an exciting pennant drive. I hoped, at least, that the Orioles (and I) would play well on those two nights when the whole world would be watching.

• September 5, 1995 •

Camden Yards was filled to the brim, and there

was a buzz in the stands. This was the day I would tie Lou Gehrig's record.

We were playing the California Angels, and it became clear from the start that my teammates were pumped up. In the second inning Chris Hoiles, Jeff Manto, Mark Smith, and Brady Anderson all slammed solo home runs. Our pitcher, Scott Erickson, was shutting out the Angels.

In the top of the fifth Brady Anderson caught the fly ball that ended the inning.

It was official. I had tied the great Lou Gehrig's record of 2,130 consecutive games.

When the big number 2,130 dropped into place, Camden Yards just exploded. *Exploded!* In our dugout there were handshakes and hugs all around. I came out for the first of many waves to the crowd. I waved to my parents, my sister Elly, and my brothers Fred and Billy.

Then I caught the eyes of Kelly, sitting in the box to the left of the dugout. All of the emotion of the year was wrapped up in these two or three seconds between Kelly and me. As I've said, baseball can be hard on a player's family. The guy is all over the country while his family is at home doing their own thing. Those few seconds of eye contact summed up a season for Kelly and me. It was a surprisingly private moment in a very public place.

After everyone calmed down, the Orioles took their at bat and I got a turn at the plate. Mark Holzemer threw me a slider and it hung. I took a rip at it.

When I connected, I didn't think I'd hit the ball hard enough to drive it out of the park. But the ball had some carry to it and dropped two rows beyond the 364 sign in left field.

What could have been better than this? I had reached Lou Gehrig's milestone and capped it off with a homer the same day. I felt great, really great. As it turned out, we scored eight runs that night and Scott Erickson pitched a shutout.

After the game I was presented with all kinds of gifts—jerseys from Hank Aaron, Ernie Banks, and Johnny Unitas. A uniform from Olympic speed-skating champion Bonnie Blair. David Letterman sent a personalized Top Ten list (reasons I need a day off).

The most touching gift of all was a baseball from Jim Gott. The same day I had started my streak— May 30, 1982—Jim had won his first big league game. He came on the field and presented me with the game ball from that day. I could hardly believe it, because "firsts" mean so much to baseball players. It was pretty amazing to me that Jim would give that ball away.

The excitement of tying Lou Gehrig's record had been incredible. I couldn't imagine that anything would ever top it. But the very next day was even *more* incredible.

• September 6, 1995 •

For one reason or another my alarm clock didn't go off that morning. It was panic time in the Ripken

household, because this was Rachel's first day of
first grade. It was a special day for both of us.

As I drove Rachel to school, we chatted about
how much fun first grade was going to be for her.
I made it a point *not* to mention that when *I* was
in first grade I'd tried to run away several times. I
didn't want to plant any ideas in her head.

Only twelve hours and one speech to go, I thought
after I dropped Rachel off.

When I got to Camden Yards that afternoon, I
was relaxed. But then I got keyed up wondering
what this night was going to be like. I wasn't feeling well. It was really hot and I was sweating. The
President and Vice-President came through the
clubhouse, and I was embarrassed to be sweating
so much.

Rachel did just fine at school. Kelly brought her
and Ryan out to the ballpark later, and both kids
got the honor of throwing out a first pitch. (Nice
pitches too, especially considering that the south-
paw, Ryan, was just two years old.) I was still
sweating. After I kissed Rachel, she wiped off the
sweat that accompanied the kiss.

I was still sweating in the bottom of the fourth
inning. We had a 2-1 lead at that point. Shawn
Boskie was on the mound and I was at bat. His
first three pitches were out of the strike zone.

I've never been much of a 3-0 hitter, and nor-
mally I would have taken the next pitch. But I had
been hitting the ball really well the last couple of
days, with good focus, concentration, and relax-

ation. I decided to give the next pitch a good swing if it was over the plate.

I stepped out of the batter's box and said to myself, *Keep your concentration. Act like it's two balls and no strikes. Calm down. See the ball.*

Boskie threw me a fastball down the middle. I nailed that pitch and I knew right away it was gone. What a thrill that was! This was extra sweet, no doubt about it.

My brother Fred told me later that he'd predicted that homer just before the pitch, and he said he'd called the one the night before too. He had that feeling, he said. My brother, the psychic.

When our second baseman Manny Alexander caught the third out in the fifth inning, the game was official. Number 2,131 dropped on the warehouse and the crowd began to cheer.

I was the new Iron Man of baseball. I had played 2,131 consecutive games. In the history of the sport, nobody had ever done that before.

What was I expecting next? I didn't know, of course. I guessed there would be a lot of cheering and curtain calls like there had been the night before. I wasn't prepared for the extent of the celebration.

First thing, I caught the eyes of my parents and waved to them. I walked over to my family's box, took off my jersey, and presented it to my kids as a way to show them I had worn a special T-shirt underneath. It said, "2130+ Hugs and Kisses for Daddy."

I figured that would be it. But when I went to

our dugout, the crowd was still screaming. Butch Burnett, one of our clubhouse guys, was just bawling. We hugged, and now I was fighting back tears myself.

I came out of the dugout and tapped my heart with my right hand. What more could I say than that? What more could I do? But the crowd wouldn't stop screaming.

"You're going to have to take a lap," my teammate Rafael Palmeiro told me. "That's the only way they'll quit."

I felt funny about that. For one thing, victory laps and other antics aren't my style. Secondly, I didn't want to disrupt the game. The Orioles may have been out of the pennant race, but the Angels were still in it. This was an important game for them, and I didn't want their pitcher Shawn Boskie to stand around for an hour.

But ten minutes after the number 2,131 was lowered, the fans were *still* going crazy. They wouldn't let the game continue. Finally, Rafael and Bobby Bonilla pushed me to the top of the dugout steps and sent me on my way around the park.

At first I just wanted to get it over with. But then, something remarkable happened. At least it seemed remarkable to me. As I jogged around the field, I looked at the people. I looked in their eyes. They were so *happy*. This moment seemed to mean as much to them as it did to me. I was overwhelmed.

So I slowed down. For a brief moment I forgot we had four more innings to play. I wanted the celebration to go on forever. Whitney Houston's "One Moment in Time" was playing over the PA system. I didn't even hear it.

As I circled the outfield and came along the third baseline, I shook hands with my brother Billy, with the umpires, and with anyone else I could reach. I wanted to shake hands with each one of the forty-six thousand people in the stands, but I couldn't reach that far.

The Angels lined up in front of their dugout and congratulated me. That was really special, because they were my peers in the game. They were in a pennant race and trying to win a game that night.

I mentioned before that there have been three incredible moments in my life—when Kelly and I got married, when Rachel was born, and when Ryan was born. This moment at Camden Yards was number four.

As I went around the field, I was almost in a dreamlike state. I was *there*, and I knew it, but it also seemed like I was somewhere off in the distance, surveying the scene.

• Thank You •

The Orioles went on to win the game, 4-2. While we were waiting for the on-field ceremony to begin, my parents and I visited in the tunnel behind the dugout. Just the three of us. Sharing the moment, pure and simple.

We didn't get into the big questions like "What did you feel out there?" Small talk about the weather is more the Ripken style. To me, actions and presence speak louder than words.

However, I also knew it was time for words from me. The crowd was waiting.

As I stepped up to the microphone, I was surprised at how relaxed I felt. I began by saying that the fans in Baltimore are the greatest, and that it was the greatest place to play. I was able to thank Mom and Dad, and Kelly, Rachel, and Ryan, without choking up. After that I thanked Eddie Murray. It was Eddie, I had long believed, who taught me how to be a major leaguer.

Finally, I paid my respects to the late Lou Gehrig, who was called on to be courageous in a way that most of us can only hope we'd measure up to.

"Some may think our greatest connection is that we both played many consecutive games," I said. "Yet I believe in my heart that the true link is the common motivation of a love of the game of baseball, a passion for your team, and a desire to compete at the very highest level. I know that if Lou Gehrig is looking down on tonight's activities, he isn't concerned with someone's playing more games than he did. Instead, he's viewing tonight as just another example of what's good and right about the great American game. Whether your name is Gehrig or Ripken, DiMaggio or Robinson, or that of some youngster who picks up his bat or puts on his glove, you are challenged by the game of baseball to do your very best, day in and day out, and that's all I've ever tried to do."

14 · The Game of Life

No matter what I do for the rest of my life, I realize that I will always be remembered for my consecutive games streak. But my life has been much more than that, and it didn't shut down once I broke Lou Gehrig's record.

In 1996, after playing 2,216 games at shortstop, I was moved to third base for a few games. (I became a permanent third baseman in 1997.)

The Orioles, after so many years of frustration, became contenders again that year. We won the American League wild card race, setting the major league record for home runs in a season. Brady Anderson hit an amazing fifty all by himself. We beat Cleveland in the playoffs before losing to the Yankees.

That was the series when a twelve-year-old kid

leaned over the wall and deflected Yankee Derek Jeter's fly ball into the stands for a "home run" that tied the game in the eighth inning. The whole series might have gone the other way if our right-fielder Tony Tarasco had been able to catch that ball. But it was the Yankees who went on to the World Series, and won it.

In 1997 we played even better as a team, and won the American League East easily. It was the first time in fourteen years that the Orioles ended a season in first place. Then we beat Seattle three out of four games (twice beating the great Randy Johnson) to advance to the American League Championship Series. We lost to Cleveland in another heartbreaker that kept us out of the World Series.

It was gratifying to see the Orioles become winners again.

I had a good beginning to the 1998 season with a grand-slam homer against Kansas City on Opening Day. In July I played in my sixteenth All-Star game in Denver. The Orioles had a slow start, then got hot for a while after the All-Star Game. Eric Davis had a thirty-game hitting streak, the longest in Orioles history. But we couldn't keep up the pace, and didn't make the playoffs.

On September 20, I took myself out of the lineup for the Orioles' last home game of the season against the Yankees. I thought the time was right to end the streak at 2,632 consecutive games.

After New York's first out, all the Yankees came

out of their dugout and tipped their hats toward me in the Orioles dugout. I tipped mine back. The crowd stood and cheered for several minutes, then I motioned to Oriole pitcher Doug Johns to throw the next pitch.

I've always believed the focus should be on the team, not the individual players, and I wanted to put the attention back where it belonged. Ending the streak hasn't changed anything about my approach to the game. My job is to play the best baseball I can.

• Looking Ahead •

Someday, I'd like the opportunity to test my knowledge and ideas. I like the idea of heading up an existing organization and trying to recapture "The Oriole Way," simply getting back to the fundamentals of baseball. If I couldn't do that, I think it would be interesting to put together an organization right from the start, like an expansion team.

It's impossible to say at this point what course I will take when my playing days are over. Kelly and I have devoted a lot of time and energy to literacy. I didn't read much when I was a boy. In the minors I discovered how much fun it is, and now I realize how crucial it is for children, and adults too. We established an adult literacy project called the Ripken Learning Center, and raised a lot of money through a program called "Reading, Runs and Ripken."

I can't say exactly what direction my life will take in the future. I won't sit around the house all day, that's for sure. I like to do things. I've focused all my energy and dedication on playing baseball for my whole adult life. I'll have to refocus on another area at some point.

In the meantime, I like the idea of developing relationships with a variety of people in many fields in order to create options for my second career. That would be typical of me: Plan, sort through, know my options before I make up my mind.

Life is like a game, they say. And whatever I do in the game of life, I'll follow the philosophy I've followed since I was a rookie sitting on a bench waiting for my chance: Play well, and play every day.

Calvin Edwin Ripken, Jr.

Born: Havre de Grace, Maryland, August 24, 1960.
Bats right, throws right. **Height:** 6'4" **Weight:** 225 lbs.

Some career statistics:

- Played 2,632 consecutive games for the Orioles, beginning his streak on May 30, 1982. He broke the major league record for the most consecutive games played on September 6, 1995, when he played his 2,131st game.

- Collected his 2,849th career hit on August 21, 1998, breaking Brooks Robinson's record for most hits by an Oriole player.

- Set a record for the most home runs ever hit by a major league shortstop when he hit his 278th homer on July 15, 1993.

- Selected Most Valuable Player in American League in 1983 and 1991. One of only twenty-three players in major league history to win the MVP award more than once.

- Received the Golden Glove Award, which recognizes the importance of superior individual fielding performance, in 1991 and 1992.

- Won the Lou Gehrig Award, which is presented annually to the Major League Baseball player who best exemplifies the giving character of Hall of Famer Lou Gehrig, in 1992.

- Holds or shares eleven major league or American League fielding records, including ML records for most consecutive errorless games (95) and highest fielding percentage in a season (.996) in 1990.

- Has made sixteen All-Star appearances.

- Played in one World Series, in 1983, which the Orioles won.

- Selected Rookie of the Year in American League, 1982.

PHOTOGRAPH CREDITS

First section:

Mickey Pfleger: page 6 (below right)

Jerry Wachter Photography Ltd: page 7 (center)

Jerry Wachter/*Sports Illustrated*: page 8 (above)

Allsport: page 8 (below)

Second section:

Jerry Wachter Photography Ltd: page 1 (above left,
below left, below right), 4 (above right)

Walter Iooss: page 1 (above right), 3 (above left, below right),
6 (below), 7 (above, center left, below left and right), 8

Walter Iooss/*Sports Illustrated*: page 2 (above left)

David Liam Kyle/*Sports Illustrated*: page 2 (above right), 5 (above right)

Chuck Solomon/*Sports Illustrated*: page 4 (below right), 6 (above)

John Iacono/*Sports Illustrated*: page 6 (center)

Allsport: page 2 (below left and right),
3 (above right, below left), 4 (above left, below left),
5 (above left, below left and right), 7 (center right)

All other photographs courtesy of the Ripken family.

The publisher would like to thank Désirée Pilachowski for
her help with this book.